AXEL HAIG

and the Victorian Vision of the Middle Ages

GENIUS OF ARCHITECTURE

Series editors: JOHN HARRIS and MARCUS BINNEY

ATHENIAN STUART *by David Watkin*
WILLIAM TALMAN *by John Harris*
AXEL HAIG *by J. Mordaunt Crook and C. A. Lennox-Boyd*
SIR ROBERT TAYLOR *by Marcus Binney*

AXEL HAIG

and the Victorian Vision of the Middle Ages

J. MORDAUNT CROOK
and
C. A. LENNOX-BOYD

London
GEORGE ALLEN & UNWIN
Boston Sydney

**George Allen & Unwin (Publishers) Ltd,
40 Museum Street, London WC1A 1LU, UK**

George Allen & Unwin (Publishers) Ltd,
Park Lane, Hemel Hempstead, Herts HP2 4TE, UK

Allen & Unwin Inc.,
9 Winchester Terrace, Winchester, Mass 01890, USA

George Allen & Unwin Australia Pty Ltd,
8 Napier Street, North Sydney, NSW 2060, Australia

First published in 1984

British Library Cataloguing in Publication Data

Crook, J. Mordaunt
Axel Haig.
1. Haig, Axel 2. Architects—Sweden—Biography
I. Title
720'.92'4 NA1293.H/
ISBN 0-04-720029-4
ISBN 0-04-720030-8 Pbk

Set in 11 on 13 point Sabon by Computape (Pickering) Ltd
and printed in Great Britain
by Mackays of Chatham

Contents

List of illustrations

Acknowledgements

Not much has been written about Axel Haig, and even less is available in English. We are therefore especially grateful to Ingele Byng and James Culverwell for translating Swedish material, and to Bengt Axel Haig for providing access to items of family history. Paul Joyce helped with information on G. E. Street and we are grateful to David Walker for unravelling at least one Scottish conundrum.

For permission to illustrate material from their collections we are grateful to the National Museum, Stockholm and the Royal Institute of British Architects (British Architectural Library, Drawings Collection); to the India Office Library, the National Trust and Worcester College, Oxford; to Miss Phyllis Lambert, Dr Michael Darby, and Commander J. Haig. Unless otherwise indicated, all illustrations of etchings by Haig are taken from the collection of C. A. Lennox-Boyd. The index was compiled on the Stipple System of Erros Computing Services Ltd., Abingdon.

J.M.C
C.A.L-B

Axel Haig and the Victorian Vision of the Middle Ages

Gothland: land of the Goths. Gothland – or Gotland as the Swedes call it – an island in the Baltic Sea, midway between Sweden and Russia, one hundred miles south of Stockholm. An island of brick and pine, and limestone cliffs; a land of runic signs and fierce sculpture, of timbered roofs and whitewashed walls; a place of windy skies and tinted sunsets, of farms and vineyards, and groves of mulberry. Gothland Gothic: this is an island with nearly one hundred medieval churches in less than a thousand square miles. Its capital is Wisby, 'the Rome of the Goths', the Nuremburg of the Baltic, a medieval stronghold crouching behind its battlements; a city of narrow streets and high-pitched roofs, thronged with battered churches and crowned by a great
cathedral [88, 104].*[1] And on the other side of this island is a **51, 53**
hamlet called Katthammarsvik, birthplace on 10 November
1835 of Axel Herman Haig[2] – the Piranesi of the Gothic Revival. **1, 2**

Like A. W. Pugin, young Haig – Hägg is the Swedish form – loved nothing better than the open sea and an open boat. His schoolboy hobbies seem to have been sketching seascapes and building model ships. His father was a small landowner and timber merchant. His brother, also an amateur artist, became an admiral in the Swedish navy.[3] For six years, sponsored by Wisby chamber of commerce, young Haig studied shipbuilding in the government dockyard at Karlskrona. Karlskrona was a dockyard with a famous history, but the future of shipbuilding lay elsewhere: in Glasgow, on the banks of the Clyde. So in 1856 Haig sailed to Scotland and for three more years he worked with the Clyde shipbuilding firm of Lawrence Hill & Co. But already

*The numbers in square brackets refer to the chronological list of prints, pp. 48–68; marginal figures in bold type refer to the illustrations.

his interests had moved on, from building boats to building houses. In his spare time at Port Glasgow he designed a residence for the head of the firm, Lawrence Hill. Now Mrs Hill had a cousin called J. Macvicar Anderson, architect to the Duke of Buccleuch, and it was Anderson who in 1859 found Haig the opening he was looking for in the London office of Ewan Christian, architect to the Ecclesiastical Commissioners. Seven years with Christian – more prolific than Gilbert Scott, and rather less interesting – taught Haig more than enough about church architecture. Seven years in Scotland Yard as an architect's draughtsman; seven years in the shadow of Mr Pecksniff. Haig's enthusiasm not only survived this experience, it was even increased. He was soon mixing with the inner circle of Gothic Revivalists. And in 1866, in Hove, Sussex – as if to mark the end of his apprenticeship – he married Sarah May, daughter of one Abrather Street. It would be nice to think that in doing so Haig had married into the Gothic Revival through an alliance with a distant cousin of G. E. Street, but that seems unlikely.

Thirty-one years of age, and newly married, Haig was now qualified in two professions – shipbuilding and architecture. But he had yet to practise either. Instead he decided to capitalise on his one undoubted skill. He became an architectural artist.

Architectural draughtsmen are a forgotten race. E. S. Cole, for example, who drew for both Burges and Butterfield, is now completely unknown. G. E. Street used to say 'Deshon is the only man in London who can draw',[4] but who now remembers F. C. Deshon? In some ways Thomas Allom was the swiftest, cleverest of them all. And where today is poor Tom Allom?

The first number of *The Architect*, on 2 January 1869, carried the following advertisements, spattered with eye-catching capitals:

> Architectural Competition Drawings, artistic tinting, designs, perspective outlines and general draughtsmanship, executed by Messrs. J. Liddell and Joseph Nash, Jun., at their own offices, no. 13, York Chambers, Adelphi, London.

A. and W. H. Lockwood, Architectural Artists and Draughtsmen, Drummond Chambers, 10, John St., Adelphi, W.C., Prepare Perspectives in Outline and Colour, and every description of Architectural Work for the Profession.

Mr. R. H. Bentham, Architect and Artist, 51 Bedford Row, W.C., makes Exterior and Interior Views for the Profession. . . .

The Advertiser (the Colourist of the First Prize Design for the Foreign Office, London, and the Government Offices, Ottawa, Canada) undertakes to do Colour Perspective and other Drawings on reasonable terms. First class Perspectives put in outline. Specimens shown. Address, Mr. Betholme, 34 Great Ormond St., Brunswick Square, W.C.

Men like these were Haig's competitors at the outset of his new career. Architects' draughtsmen – then as perhaps now – had a status little higher than tradesmen. J. Drayton Wyatt – 'Scott's Wyatt' as he was known, because he drew out so many of Sir Gilbert Scott's designs – was blackballed at the Society of Antiquaries.[5]

From 1867 onwards Haig's name appears regularly on illustrations in architectural papers, first *The Building News*, then *The Architect*. Rowand Anderson and John Burnet employed him in Scotland; Worthington employed him in Manchester; Lockwood and Mawson employed him in Bradford; and – to list only the best known names – Burges, Godwin, Brooks, Street, Prichard and Emerson all employed him in London. At times, in the 1870s, he seems almost to rank as accredited draughtsman to half the profession. When, for example, a sensational view of
Bombay Railway Station – the Victoria Terminus (1879–86)[6] – 25
appeared at the Royal Academy in 1880, the architect was F. W. Stevens, but the artist was Axel Haig. Haig was indeed every
architect's friend. But one name stands out: William Burges 3, 4
became not only Haig's first major employer but also his ally for life. Perhaps it was compatibility of temperament: both men were jocular, easygoing extroverts. Just possibly it was their

mutual interest in Freemasonry.[7] More likely, it was simply congruity of interest: Burges needed an artist who could capture his vision of the medieval world; Haig needed a patron who could pay.

1866–7 was the turning-point: the year of the great competition for London's new Law Courts in the Strand. Together with E. W. Godwin and R. Phéné Spiers, Haig worked feverishly on Burges's competition design, perhaps the most amazing conception in the history of the Gothic Revival. When Haig's perspective views went on show in Lincoln's Inn Fields, Burges's cloud-capped towers were an immediate sensation. The eventual winner, G. E. Street, is said to have exclaimed: 'I wouldn't mind being beaten by drawings like those.' The conception belonged to Burges; some of the details belonged to Godwin; the Strand elevation drawing belonged to Phéné Spiers. But those spectacular bird's-eye views those sensational worm's-eye perspec-
14 tives, were the work of Axel Herman Haig.[8]

The Law Courts competition marked the start of a long and fruitful association between Haig and Burges, broken only by the latter's death in 1881. In 1870 it was Haig who prepared
15 Burges's panoramic perspective of Knightshayes, Devon.[9] In the
same year it was Haig who supplied views of Lord Bute's bizarre
winter smoking room in the clock tower at Cardiff Castle,
10 complete with figures dressed in medieval garb. [10] In 1871 it was
16, 17 the semi-circular Speech Room at Harrow School.[11] In 1872 it
13 was Burges's designs for Mr McConnochie's house at Cardiff,[12]
and the exquisite Yorkshire churches of Skelton,[13] and Studley
23 Royal.[14] In 1873 Haig prepared, on Burges's behalf, a watercolour advertisement for grandiose buildings at Trinity College,
22 Hartford, Conn.[15] and a watercolour temptation for the Fellows
of Worcester College, Oxford, showing their dining hall as it
18 might be[16] – they had already fallen for a similarly tempting view
prior to Burges's transmogrification of their chapel.[17] 1873 was also the year of two more watercolour spectaculars by Haig: Burges's competition designs for St Mary's Cathedral, Edinburgh.[18] And a year later came one of the sensations of the 1874 Royal Academy show: Burges's scheme for the grand staircase at Cardiff Castle.[19]

But Haig's most dramatic work for Burges was still to come.

At the Royal Academy Exhibition of 1875 Burges exhibited three
staggering designs for the interior decoration of St Paul's Cathedral: the dome, the chancel and a general view.[20] All were 26
large-scale watercolour perspectives, and all by Haig. Such was
their impact that the public outcry against any tampering with
Wren's masterpiece was almost stifled – almost, but not quite. At
the Paris International Exhibition of 1878,[21] Burges exhibited
three more designs: the clock tower at Cardiff Castle; the
Chancel at Studley Royal, Yorkshire; and the Bishop's throne at
St Finbar's Cathedral, Cork.[22] Again, all were watercolour per- 21
spectives, and all by Haig. In 1879 Haig prepared a delightful
view of Burges's 'Swiss' bridge over the moat of Cardiff Castle. 11
Finally, in 1880, came the library of Burges's own fantastic
retreat, Tower House, Melbury Road, Kensington.[23] Billy 24
Burges, the architect of a medieval dreamland, had found an
artist worthy of his dreams.

Certainly Haig revered Burges's memory all his life. Something
of the fantastic element in Burges's drawings – the 'Sabrina
Fountain' (1856),[24] 'St Simeon Stylites' (1860)[25] – surfaces from 8
time to time in Haig's visionary views: 'The Legend of the Bells'
(1895) [136], for instance. As late as 1891 Haig reminded an
audience of student architects:

> One of the most fertile figure-draughtsmen I have known was ... an architect. ... So ready was he in composition, and so sure in drawing, that he could, straight off, without previous pencilling, quickly fill a sheet of paper with lovely design, correctly wrought out in pen and ink, were the intricacies of groups or ornament ever so astounding. But he was a phenomenon, and he himself, and his world, regretted that his field of labour was so limited. Very versatile, he was one of the few great examples of what some of the renaissance men must have been. Honour and peace to his ashes, for he was a great draughtsman.[26]

Years later, Sir Reginald Blomfield – never a friend of the Goths – had to admit: 'Burges could have drawn anything, if only he could have forgotten that he was a medievalist.'[27]

Burges's designs established Haig as the best known – and

most admired – architectural artist of his day. 'If anyone', noted the *Church Builder*, can 'throw [a] kind of glamour over … architectural features … it is Mr Haig, … one of our most experienced and most artistic architectural draughtsmen and colourists.'[28] He was never exclusively employed by Burges: in 1868, for instance, Haig was the draughtsman chosen by Street to draw out his church of St John, Torquay, for publication;[29] and in the late 1870s Street employed him to produce an interior perspective of the Guards' Chapel at Wellington Barracks, London.[30] In 1868 Haig published a view of Sir George Lea's half-timbered 'Old English' house at Bagshot, Surrey: architects Walford and Donkin.[31] In 1869 came the Bristol Assize Courts: architects Popes and Bindon;[32] E. P. Shirley's Ettington Park Warwicks.: architect John Prichard;[33] and Bradford Town Hall: architects Lockwood and Mawson.[34] In 1870 it was St Andrew, Plaistow: architect James Brooks.[35] All these take the form of lithographic plates made from Haig's drawings. Some of his sketches at this time – Barningham Hall and Barsham Hall, Norfolk, for example – were taken from photographs and are really hack work, no better than the productions of forgotten draughtsmen like F. W. Roper or H. Abbot. They were not made to be scrutinised too carefully. In any case their function proved ephemeral. With the development of photolithography in the 1870s, such mechanical operations became obsolete.

At this stage of his career Haig seems to have been content to act as a kind of architectural mercenary, advertising the wares of underemployed colleagues, 'cooking' drawings for 'competition wallahs'. As he later admitted, he was forced to become an expert in the production of 'meretricious drawings', designed, 'with a certain pretty coquetry', to 'throw dust in the eyes of honest clients'.[36]

Like Burges and Godwin, Haig always distinguished between architectural drawings and drawings of architecture: architectural drawings should be essentially diagrammatic and explanatory; drawings of architecture might deviate into pictorial representation.[37] 'The former', Haig explained, 'represents a thing as it really is, the other as it appears. … One [is] preparatory … the other mostly retrospective or … creative. … Both may … be equally artistic. … For the picture, planes and light and shade; for the diagram, firm outlines. . . . The difficulty arises when the two methods are confused.' Hence the fact that 'the architectural artist . . . has to subdue his intelligence . . . and . . . show only what he sees'. If he tries to include details which are normally invisible – say for purposes of advertisement – he will destroy the artistic content of the drawing. In his days as a hack, Haig later confessed, it was often his 'lot . . . to make drawings in that manner, always under protest; but . . . never . . . again'.[38]

During this 'hack' phase, Haig had also begun to exhibit drawings under his own name. At the Royal Academy he made his debut in 1870 with a watercolour called 'The Quiet Hour'.[39] This was followed in 1871 by 'Fulham from Putney Bridge – early spring effect'.[40] Thereafter, in 1874, 1876, 1877 and 1879 he exhibited half a dozen sketches – Limburg, Pompeii, Nuremburg, Palermo, Verona and Loches – all trophies of foreign travel.[41] The next stage of his career – as a roving pictorial topographer – had begun.

In 1875 Haig set out – at Burges's suggestion – for Sicily. Burges had told him of the glories of Monreale [212] and the Capella Palatina [187]. Now he was to see for himself. Riding donkeys, and escorted by soldiers, Mr and Mrs Haig explored the Concha d'Oro. Installed in a former Benedictine monastery – in the abbot's apartments no less – they struck up friendship with the officers of the Bersaglieri. Palermo became their headquarters. And the splendours of Siculo-Norman art more than fulfilled their expectations.

Like Burges, Haig never forgot Palermo. Its great cathedral, Saracenic Romanesque; the mosaics of the Capella Palatina, glittering in incense gloom; the coloured cupolas of the Martorana; the quintuple domelets of the Eremiti – here were the treasures of successive civilisations, mingled together in glorious confusion. And those Sicilians!

> Stretching along the coast at the foot of the town is the Marina, with the Mediterranean on one side and terraces and Palatial buildings on the other, with the view of Monte Pellegrino in one direction, and the rocky coast towards Cephalu on the other. . . . The crowd is vast, full of fiery elements, and yet very orderly. Who shall say that the worst

> brigand in Sicily may not be there, enjoying his sorbetto, his glass of marsala or his cigaretto, side by side with his enemy the dashing bersagliere, his victim the wealthy merchant, or his occasional friend and adviser the priest. All are apparently enjoying themselves, deservedly or not, after a day of hard work or one of idleness, under the well-nigh tropical sun – a sight that none but the misanthrope can grumble at. ... There are thieves in the best regulated communities ... but if I had the choice I would rather be cheated ... in Palermo than in Naples ... or almost any town I know.

If Haig possessed even a hint of Scandinavian reserve, it seems to have melted in Sicilian sunshine. We catch him laughing at the sight of fireworks in the moonlight. He even chuckles at the expletives of the native priests: the sound of 'el diabolo', for instance, emerging from the 'thick lips' of a Palermitan prelate.[42]

After three months in Sicily, Haig headed home via Naples and Rome, visiting on the way the major towns of north Italy: Florence, Pisa, Bologna, Verona and – inevitably – Venice. Then northwards again, through the Tyrol to Germany. His objective now – again on Burges's advice – was Nuremburg. This was Haig's first visit to 'the Oxford of Germany'. Here he found inspiration that would last him many years. His sketches of streets and houses, castles and churches later supplied specific material for a number of celebrated views.[43] And it was Nuremburg which eventually provided the background for his
27 first major visionary etching, 'The Vesper Bell' (1879) [18].

At this stage, of course, Haig had yet to take up etching. Pencil sketches and luminous watercolours were his forte. But this long journey – like Burges's long journey in 1853–4 – had laid the visual foundations for his later fame as a topographical etcher. Meanwhile, the fruits of his travels were appearing regularly in the architectural press. From 1878 to 1880 date views of Pisa[44] and Genoa;[45] Bologna[46] and Siena;[47] Azay-le-Rideau,[48] Lisieux[49] and Malines;[50] Loches,[51] Bourges[52] and Cologne.[53] Each of these displays the brilliant compositional technique which was already Haig's trademark, even though he modestly described at least one – 'A Street in Bruges' (1880) – as 'a chance sketch, taken at random, during ... a stroll'.

In a sense, Haig had to make his reputation three times over: as an architect's draughtsman, as a watercolourist, and as an etcher. By the late 1870s he was acknowledged to be the ablest architectural artist in Britain, as well as a topographical watercolourist of no mean talent. But his third career – as an etcher – had only just begun.

* * *

Haig's first attempts at etching date from 1877.[54] Among his earliest experiments in the new medium were views of a windmill
like one near his old home at Katthammarsvik [1] and a distant 1
view of Verona [19]. It was Rowand Anderson who seems to have prompted this change of artistic direction. Anderson was an able eclectic, but a notoriously poor draughtsman. He first employed Haig in the preparation of his *Examples of Municipal, Commercial and Street Architecture of France and Italy, 12th–15th century* (1862).[55] A few years later Anderson projected a volume on Scottish medieval architecture, to be illustrated with etchings. This book never appeared: Anderson was already fully occupied on Lord Bute's Gothic palace at Mount Stuart. But proof etchings, of Linlithgow [7, 9, 10], Melrose [16], Jedburgh [21] and Holyrood [8, 12], indicate Haig's early mastery of this newly adopted process.

Haig's arrival as an etcher was marked by four successive exhibits at the Royal Academy: 'The Morning of the Festival'
(1880) [24];[56] 'Chartres Cathedral: in the Aisles' (1881) [30];[57] 30
'Chartres, under the great north porch' (1882) [36];[58] and 'Peterborough Cathedral' (1883) [42].[59] First as a watercolourist, then 37
as a painter-etcher, he had now broken into the sacred groves of Burlington House. After that, he could afford to divide his talents along commercial lines: his watercolours continued to appear at the Royal Academy;[60] his etchings were snapped up by shops and galleries in half the capitals of Europe.

Now the wonder of all engraving, all etching, lies in its infinite precision; its magic in its multiplicability. Let Ruskin explain the mystery:

> Look close at that engraving – imagine it to be a drawing in pen and ink, and yourself required similarly to produce its parallel! . . . take your pen – your finest – and just try to copy the leaves that entangle the nearest cow's head . . . take a strong magnifying glass . . . count the dots and lines that gradate the nostrils and the edges of the facial bone . . . examine it well, and then – I humbly ask of you – try to do a piece of it yourself! . . . do the merely etched outline yourself, if no more. Look you – you hold your etching needle this way, as you would a pencil, nearly; and then – you etch with it! it is as easy as lying . . . count how many lines there are in a laurel bush – in an arch – in a casement: some hundred and fifty, or two hundred, deliberately drawn lines . . . in every square quarter of an inch; – say *three thousand to the inch*, – each with skilful intent put in its place! and then consider what the ordinary sketcher's work must appear to the men who have been trained to this! . . . And this scratch or inscription of yours will be seen of a multitude of eyes. It is not like a single picture or a single wall painting; this multiplicable work will pass through thousand thousand hands, strengthen and inform innumerable souls, if it be worthy; vivify the folly of thousands if unworthy. . . . This engraving will not be gossiped over and fluttered past at private views of academies; listlessly sauntered by in corners of great galleries. Ah, no! This will hang over parlour chimney-pieces – shed down its hourly influence on children's forenoon work. This will hang in little luminous corners by sick beds; mix with flickering dreams by candlelight, and catch the first rays from the window's 'glimmering square'. You had better put something good into it![61]

For Ruskin, however, etching always took second place to line-engraving. 'Etching', he concluded, 'is the very refuge and mask of sentimental uncertainty, and of vigorous ignorance. If you know anything clearly, and have a firm hand, depend upon it, you will draw it clearly; and you will not care to hide it among scratches and burrs. And herein is the . . . grand distinction between etching and engraving – that in the etching needle you have an almost irresistible temptation to wanton speed.'[62] Well, maybe. But if so it was a temptation which Haig amply resisted. Never was the etching needle used with greater care.

The mid-Victorian revival of etching might be said to date from 1860. That was the year in which Sir F. Seymour Haden exhibited, under the nom de plume 'H. Deane', the first original – as opposed to reproduction – etching at the Royal Academy. Twenty years later in 1880 it was Haden – etcher, surgeon and autocrat – who founded the Royal Society of Painter-Etchers and Engravers. Haig, by now almost middle-aged, became one of its founder-members.[63] The Society – 'Royal' from 1898 – was founded largely because etchers were consistently excluded from Burlington House, even though line-engravers were admitted. Apart from Haden's inspiration and Hamerton's instruction – his handbook *Etchings and Etchers* (1865), his publicity in *The Portfolio* – another important factor in the re-establishment of etching was the success of the 'Black and White' Exhibitions at the Dudley Gallery and the Egyptian Hall. Across the Channel, taste had already changed. Corot, Jacque, Millet, Lalanne, Méryon, Jacquemart, Bracquemond – the French school of etchers were already well established.[64] In England, therefore, in the 1870s, Whistler and Haden were selling on a rising market.[65] Photography had killed the arduous art of line-engraving. But etching and woodcut flourished. 'Photographs and chromo-lithographs had both had their day, and the time was ripe for a novelty; and when, moreover, it was found that etchings in black frames suited the modern 'art' furniture, the success of the revival was assured.'[66] Etchings replaced line-engravings as a popular art-form, reproductive and original. Copper etching plates themselves were even used as drawing-room decoration. Haig's arrival as an etcher could hardly have been better timed.

As an etcher, Haig was essentially self-taught. P. G. Hamerton's writings must have been his bible. A painstaking, methodical worker, his technique was slow to develop. As a boy in Gothland he had first been taught to draw by P. A. Säve. Then, like Muirhead Bone after him, he had trained as an architect long before he became an etcher. His energy must have been inexhaustible. First the travel and the pencil sketches; then the detailed drawing or watercolour; then the labour of the etching itself; and finally, perhaps, a few touches of drypoint or aquatint – the whole sequence often stretching over several years. Early on, he mastered the reverse process: he habitually produced his etchings without the aid of a mirror. And he seems to have had no need of an easel: his sketches were made in street or courtyard, 'standing ... with his drawing-block or book resting on his left forearm ... in a busy street, imperturbable and absorbed amid the passers-by'.[67] Quality apart, the sheer volume of his work is impressive. A retrospective exhibition at The Fine Art Society, London, in 1904 included no less than 140 pencil drawings and 136 framed etchings.[68] In New York in 1919, sales of the Hood and Boland collections listed 218 and 230 etchings respectively. And in his own *Who's Who* entry Haig claimed to have published over 400.

Of course he had his weaknesses. Haig's figures are nearly
33 always wooden; his foliage – in 'Haddon' (1880) [28] or 'Peter-
37 borough Cathedral' (1883) [42] for instance[69] – seldom matches
his masterly evocation of masonry. But in most respects his
technique is dazzling, not only in etching proper but in drypoint
– as in 'Burgos from the River' (1896) [144] or 'Toledo' (1884)
56 [49] – and in aquatint – as in 'On the Arlanzon, near Burgos'
46 (1894) [134] or 'Cologne' (1886) [66]. His technical progression
was swift. He starts in 1877 with messy aquatint or a simple
linear silhouette. After 1879 he uses the burr freely to emphasise
28 tone (for example 'Caen', 1879) [20]. After 1881 he adds an acid
tone (for example 'Chartres', 1881 [29]) to give a richness large etchings often lack. From 1888 he adds the then unfashionable medium of aquatint to improve the contrasts. And in the 1890s he is still experimenting with line-engraving, drypoint and lithography. Not until 1910 does his virtuosity of hand and eye begin to fail. But by then he was seventy-five years of age. Finally, it was Haig's good fortune to find a printer who could do full justice to his technique: Frederick Goulding, one of the greatest of plate-printers, a man whose work rivals that of Auguste Delatre.

Before 1879 Haig was hardly known outside Burges's circle of
27 Goths. In that year, however, 'The Vesper Bell' [18] suddenly
made him famous. It was one of Burges's closer friends, Tom Taylor[70] – dramatist and art critic of *The Times* – who really made Haig's name. In an article of 1880 entitled 'More about Etchings',[71] he reviewed the 1879 Black and White Exhibition at

the Dudley Gallery, and compared Haig's first work – to Haig's advantage – with that of much better known figures such as R. W. Macbeth, Paul Rajon, Charles Méryon, Hubert Herkomer, C. F. Slocombe, Brunet-Debaines and others. The chief subject of his praise was, of course, 'The Vesper Bell':

> The subject ... represents the approach up several flights of intricate stairway to a German cathedral, the ridge-pinnacles of which, cut against the skyline, are broken by a transept-gable and a belfry turret in which the vesper bell is swinging its summons. Over the deeply recessed gateway runs a covered passage surmounted like a rood loft by a crucifix. On either side the gate, struck by the sidelong light of eventide, rise richly-decorated flanking pavilions with statued and pinnacled niches, angle-turrets, clusters of peaked roofs, deep cornices with armorial bearings in stone, and below, a shafted oriel and richly canopied doors and windows, the lines of architecture broken by the leafy branches of a tall elm. ... Up the steps leading to the gateway cloaked and coifed worshippers wend their way to vespers, the light falling here and there on wimpled head or white-robed shoulder. The scene might be Nuremburg; the period that of Dürer. ... Fault may, doubtless, be found here and there with details of light and shadow, very difficult to avoid in so intricate a composition. Elaboration is carried to a length which the advocates of extempore work in etching would very likely condemn as beyond the right limits of the art. Leaving this point for the discussions of experts, we are content with frankly admiring the extraordinary command of all the etcher's means shown in this most striking plate, and the resulting richness of tone and picturesqueness of character and effect.

Haig quickly capitalised on this success. In 1880 'A Quiet
Hour' [25] was exhibited at the Dudley Gallery,[72] and a com- 31
panion piece to 'The Vesper Bell' was issued entitled 'The
Morning of the Festival' [24]. 'It is a large work', noted *The* 30
Etcher, 'full of life and movement, and the architectural details
are rendered with great accuracy.'[73] True enough. But there is

more to it than that. Like 'The Vesper Bell', 'The Morning of the Festival' demonstrates supremely well Haig's one overriding talent: his gift for eclectic composition.

Two years before, Haig had already appeared in *The Etcher* with 'A Corner at Huy, on the Meuse' [23] – a celebration of just one of the picturesque cities along that 'gem of rivers'.[74] And in 1881 the *Art Journal*, in the person of its editor, Marcus B. Huish, finally gave the Swedish artist its imprimatur. With
32 subjects like 'An Old German Mill' (1880) [26], noted Huish, 'Mr. Haig ... has sprung into fame as an etcher of some plates of highly imaginative character, especially ... [those] piles of buildings which he has reared up in the backgrounds of the scenes.' Here Haig had managed to distil his 'collected reminiscences' of Germany into one or two highly charged compositions. Here was an etcher capable of 'expression, originality, personality'.[75]

Clearly Haig had struck a chord in the aesthetic consciousness of a generation. How did he do it? When 'An Old Hanse Town'
38 [45] appeared in the *Art Journal* for 1883, Cosmo Monkhouse felt obliged to produce an explanation:

> There are few artists ... who have made so swift a reputation in England.... [In just] three years ... he has become as popular as any.... He was *bienvenu* from the first, and it is saying nothing derogatory to his quality as an artist, to add that the cause of his favourable reception by the public must not only be looked for in his skill. ... An artist who is to succeed promptly must draw what the public likes. ... Etching and sketching are brothers, but the public like a 'picture' with finish and body in it, to hang on their walls; and that is what Mr. Haig has supplied them with.... He has given us etchings which combine much of the completeness of a steel engraving with the tone, the colour, and the vital touch of a pen-and-ink drawing.... The feeling of Mr. Haig's etching is one peculiarly grateful to the present generation of men whose life is at such high pressure, and when leisure is so scant. In the contrast with modern life lies their charm to the busy dweller in the metropolis. To see one of his pictures is like turning from a crowded street into a cathedral close.... [There is] beauty ... [and] age ... [as

> well as] associations ... [in] these strange pictures of old places on the Continent. It is not only change of air, say the doctors, that does so much good, but change of scene and life, change complete. To those who have no great sensibility for picturesqueness or medieval sentiment, Mr. Haig's etchings will convey at least something of a holiday feeling, and arouse both memory and expectation; but there are few even among the untravelled and uneducated who do not like what with affectionate tautology they call the 'old, ancient places'.[76]

When 'A Street in Cologne' [105] appeared as the frontispiece in the *Art Journal* of 1892, C. Lewis Hind took up the same theme as Monkhouse and drew in comparisons with the 'Interior of Burgos' [80], 'A Moorish Archway, Toledo' [48] and 'Chartres **50**
Street Scene and Cathedral' [37]. **36**

> It is but a few years ... since Mr. Haig ... set a new fashion with these tall, strong plates ... [and] embarked, almost by accident, on the career he now follows so patiently, so lucratively, and with such distinction. ... His first plate, 'The Vesper Bell', which issued from his studio in June 1879, was fit and ready for victory, and it took popularity with such a leap that the etcher felt justified in giving up all else. ... Great masters of the needle had been before, great masters were still alive, but it was not Mr. Haig's fate to challenge comparison with them. His was a new method – individual, personal; a method which never so much as even looked askance at impressionism. He was possessed by a feeling for minute and accurate detail, wedded to a power of broad, bold treatment, and that rare gift of imbuing with mystery and romance things in which other men see only the commonplace. ... He had a new thing to say ... he said it excellently well, and he reaped his reward. ... Mr. Haig's method is not to begin and finish a plate at a single sitting, content to have recorded one brilliant and suggestive impression of a scene; rather is he the worker – patient and accurate, building slowly line by line. With Meissonier he possesses that infinite capacity for taking pains which

> Carlyle defined as genius; but he has also that 'something else' without which the most splendidly industrious craftsman is always the exemplary workman – and no more. . . . Mr. Haig is not always the etcher of dim interiors, where holy statues stand sentinel, and worshippers steal on tip-toe across the tessellated pavements: sometimes he darts off to a scene of light and colour and bustle, anxious over the composition rather than the architecture, as witness the Cairo series; while for sunshine – diffused, sparkling – who could devise a better example than the Moorish archway?. . .
>
> In his appreciation and his understanding of cities 'half as old as time', their tortuous ways, their unrestrained buildings, their great cathedrals, in his power of reproducing the majesty and the mystery that stays always by them, lies some of the secret of Mr. Haig's success. . . . His work calls a street-bred race to the knowledge of a wider world; of a past, alongside which the present, engrossing and sufficient though it be, is but a single incident in a long journey; of other customs, other adventures. . . . To those whom fortune has given the leisure to experience these things, the Haig etchings are mementoes; to those who have seen no city but their own, they are an earnest of life's possibilities.[77]

Haig's drawings set out to be archaeological records; his etchings, on the other hand, were essentially 'pictorial, and . . . necessitated a good deal of composition'.[78] This selective vision – compositional eclecticism – is summed up by his towering view of St Ours, at Loches, in Touraine:

> The view I have selected is unusual, and has, as far as I know, not been photographed; indeed the photographer would have to cut down a tree or two to get at it. . . . The subject . . . was exceedingly beautiful in the clear moonlight of an evening in October, the church standing out in an opalescent light against a dark starspangled sky, all the objects in the foreground being in deep mysterious shadow, with a lit-up window or doorway here and there. In fact the

> scene, illuminated by sun or moon, is one not easily forgotten.[79]

His object was Romantic truth, not photographic precision. If necessary, he could rival Hollar for accuracy. But 'Mr. Haig', noted *The Times* in 1882, 'does not guarantee absolute accuracy ... he is not certain that while contemplating [Chartres] by night he did not imagine things which have no existence in reality.'[80] Haig's compositions, in fact, are almost invariably eclectic: his 'Street in Cologne' (1891) [105], for instance, achieves its pictorial impact by a careful process of selection and rejection. So too with his details: the carving on a pillar in the interior of Amiens (1893) [118], for example, is derived from the altar of St Riquier, near Abbeville. 'Inventing half my subject as I do,' he admitted, 'I can claim to be correct only in representing those monuments of old which are so beautiful that it would be impertinent of any modern man to try to improve them; but in order to make a picture in which even these fine old subjects may occur, much has to be altered in accessories and surroundings.'[81]

In a sense, Haig's visionary views are travel brochures for a world of dreams: Victorian visions of the Middle Ages, but the Middle Ages as they might have been, the Middle Ages by
moonlight. Was Limburg [62] ever quite like that?[82] Or Chartres **43**
[29, 37]? 'Solid as stone', noted the *Athenaeum*; 'stupendous **36**
sublimity ... repose, gathering shadows, and the sinking splendours of afternoon ... [with] sunlight suffusing the smoky air'.[83] But even Chartres was never quite so sublime. Haig's selective eclecticism has rearranged the cathedral's setting to suit his own perspective. 'This etching', commented the *Art Journal*, 'should induce many tourists to go out of their way this next summer to visit this wonderful city and cathedral. We cannot give a higher tribute to Mr. Haig's etching than to say they will probably be disappointed in not finding such a medieval scene as they expect.'[84]

'Mont St Michel' (1882) [35] still more. Haig was determined **35**
to emphasise the 'lonely grandeur' of that rocky pile looming out across 'the treacherous pathless sand'. He waded out at low tide, and actually prepared his sketches to the 'distant roar' of the incoming waves. The result was a triumph of selective imagi-

nation. 'Mont St Michel', noted *The Times*, displayed all the
artist's 'technical skill, his mastery of light and shade, and his
power of combining breadth of effort with regard for slight,
though not unimportant detail'.[85] Here indeed is drama and
gloom. Still more so in his sensational views of Zwingenburg
45, 44 [65] and Segovia [63]: what Ruskin memorably described as 'the
loneliness . . . of the medieval baron, nested on his solitary jut of
crag ... in lion-like isolation; the village inhabited by his
retainers straggling indeed about the slopes of the rocks at his
feet, but his own dwelling standing gloomily apart, between
them and the incomparable clouds, commanding from sunset to
sunrise, the flowing flame of some calm unvoyaged river, and the
endless undulation of the untraversable hills'.[86]

1882, the year of 'Mont St Michel', was also the year of
another etching of quite a different nature: 'Darwin's Study'
[38]. Here Haig's customary virtuosity is employed for quite a
different purpose: to record a shrine, yes; but this time it is a
secular shrine, a shrine to the apostle of evolution. The tension at
the heart of the High Victorian dream – a vision of the future
mirrored dimly in a vision of the past – could hardly be better
illustrated. Still, not a sign of this tension appears in any of Haig's
published writings: his descriptive notes give never a hint of
doubt.

Many of Haig's etchings and lithographs were accompanied
by descriptive letterpress. Dunthorne's brochures for 'Mont St
Michel' [39, 40] and 'Chartres' [31] were particularly elaborate.
Haig's written style tended to be ornate, almost as overwrought
as his art. But occasionally he hits the right note. His *Impressions*
41 *of Westminster Abbey* (1885) [51–3, 58–61], for instance,
evokes in verbal as well as pictorial images 'the beautiful
arcading, glorious with delicate carving' – and points out the
incongruity of classical statues like that of Sir Robert Peel,
looking for all the world 'like a Roman senator posing in the
frigidarium of a Roman bath'.[87] And at Amiens, writing in the
cathedral itself, 'in the cold and darkness of November 1893',
Haig did more than justice to 'the boldness of the vertical lines,
the continuity of the horizontal ones, the lightness and elegance
of the columns, the curve of the vaulting ... the temperate
richness of the details ... the straightforward simplicity of the

whole'. Here he felt borne in on him 'the soul and conscience of art'.[88]

Much of the lure of Gothic – the magical appeal of the Middle Ages – lay in the gloom and grandeur of ancient ruins, in the mystery of 'olden time'. Now Ruskin regarded etching – almost as much as woodcut – as a medium uniquely suitable for the portrayal of gloom.[89] 'It is the peculiar character of etching', he explained, 'that it cannot render beauty. You may hatch and scratch your way to picturesqueness or to deformity – never to beauty. You can etch an old woman, or an ill-conditioned fellow. But you cannot etch a girl – nor, unless in old age, or with a very partial rendering of him, a gentleman. And thus ... there is always a tendency in etchers to fasten on unlovely objects; and the whole scheme of modern rapid work of this kind is connected with a peculiar gloom which results from the confinement of men ... in ... foul and vicious cities.'[90] Hence the horror of Gustave Doré. And hence the Gothic sublimity of Axel Herman Haig.

Ruskin's ideal etching was very different from Haig's. Ruskin preferred a performance based on purity of line. He grew to hate variations in tone, 'gradations in bite', and all the other 'tricks of the etching trade'.[91] 'The virtue of an etching', he believed, 'is to express perfectly harmonious sense of light and shade, but not to realise it. All fine etchings are done with few lines.'[92] Many disagreed. P. G. Hamerton, for instance, could point to Haden and Samuel Palmer as etchers who had mastered the divine art of chiaroscuro.[93] And even Ruskin had to admit that the art of etching – like that of mezzotint – was capable of triumphant variations of texture: most of all, that glorious 'darkness ... bloomy, or velvety, as of a rose-leaf, or peach'.[94] Among these masters of darkness, no etcher was darker than Haig. Shadowy vaults and flickering lights; the inky vastness of Burgos [80, 211, 50
224];[95] the long-drawn aisles of Amiens [118, 148] the half-lit sanctuary at Durham [119]; the sombre majesty of Palencia [143] or Toledo [233]; the sunbeams piercing the chilly light of Ulm [177]; or the tapers flaring in the darkling caverns of Assisi [183]. The contrasts are sometimes excessive.[96] But as an interpreter, and populariser, of monumental architecture, Haig ranked – with the late Victorian public at least – almost as the Piranesi of Gothic.

Maurice B. Adams summed him up as follows: Haig was a master of 'brush, lithographic pen, needle or pencil ... he ... made no claim to compete with painters, but his architectural draughtsmanship ranks without a doubt among the foremost of his time, whether abroad or at home, and in some respects his graphic capability remains unique'.[97] In pen and pencil sketches, in watercolour, in etching, Haig's almost 'scientific precision' was linked to the most vivid of Romantic imaginations. As early as 1871 a fellow Swede, F. W. Scholander, had identified this combination of talents as unique: 'He really is amazingly skilled in architectural drawing. ... [By comparison] other people are ... merely indulging their own empty imaginations.' Here was archaeology turned fantastic: 'the dead monuments live again; the light plays amongst spires and turrets, and streams through rose windows over tiny, devout figures, and shadows creep under the arches of bridges and arcades, everything combines to create a mood'.[98] The Gothic world is the source of inspiration. But its ingredients have been filtered through the eye of an artist born in the age of Ruskin.

Haig's travels – even apart from his annual trips to Gothland – were formidably energetic. Like some neo-Viking of the graphic arts, he scoured Europe in search of architectural treasure, returning from each voyage laden with sketches: Belem [200] and Bruges [22]; Arles [78] and Verona [17, 176]. From Caen [20][99] to Constantinople [270][100] from Orebro [55] in the north to Barcelona [87, 164] and Busaco [204] in the south; from the towers of Vitré [184] to 'the devil's aquaduct' at Segovia[101] and the 'quaint, diabolical monstrosities' on the portals of Santiago [195];[102] from the crowded alleys of Cairo [102] or Seville [57] to the glitter of Monreale [212] and the flickering tracery of Bourges [236] or Rheims [110] – wherever he went, there was
55 material for the eclectic eye. 'Castle Nowhere' (1892) [113], for instance. The lair of the lost Viking? Fortress, perhaps, of Ruskin's solitary knight – 'master of some mountain promontory in the green recesses of Northern Europe, watching ... the lightning of the lonely sea flash round the sands of Harlech, or the mists changing their shapes for ever, among the changeless pines that fringe the crests of Jura'.[103] 'The Vesper Bell', 'The Morning of the Festival', 'A Quiet Hour', 'The Fountain of St

George' (1885) [54], 'Towing in the Prize' (1891) [104]: Haig's **40, 53** reputation rested, and will continue to rest, on that key, ambivalent gift, his talent – or weakness – for turning archaeology into art. In this respect he stands four square with the architects of the Gothic Revival. Their success is his success; their failure is his failure. In the art of Axel Herman Haig are many of the strengths and weaknesses of the Victorian vision of the Middle Ages.

In a sense, the Victorians simply knew too much. Paul Waterhouse explained the problem in 1896:

> The present century has been pre-eminently the age of the sketch-book.... Our Gothic Revivalists scoured Europe for Gothic ammunition, and the creators whose activity adorned Regent's Park and Fitzroy Square dug ores in Greece or remote Spalato. ... More recently, and with less transfiguration in the process, the sketch-book has borne its cargoes back from the brick miracles of Bruges and Nuremburg, and from the placid wharves of Holland. Even Spain ... has at last been forced into contribution. ... [All] the phases of our shifting styles have [had] their reflex in ... changes of hunting ground. ... You can hardly visit a building of beauty anywhere in Europe without the discouraging sense as you pull out sketch-book and pencil that all you see ... and every detail of it, has been already recorded and published, and probably much better drawn than you can draw it yourself.... But is the sketch-book therefore to die? Never, and for these reasons. Primarily, because in architecture the pencil works with the brain, and the brain with the pencil. To draw is to learn.... Never draw to make a pretty sketch-book – Burges taught us that. ... We ... sketch ... for the training of our hands, the strengthening of our memories, and the cultivation of the nameless and indefinable faculty which is the mainspring of art.[104]

Well, perhaps. But too many Victorians – artist and architect alike – lacked the talent to transcend their own sources of inspiration. The magic of the Middle Ages was just too potent.

Haig certainly followed the Keatsian principle of composition:

'load every rift with ore'. Each dream picture is a veritable anthology. The spires of Chartres appear in 'A Quiet Hour' (1880) and reappear in 'A Street in France' (1880) [27]. Rothenburg, Bavaria, forms the setting for 'The Fountain of St George' (1885), as does Nuremburg for 'The Vesper Bell' (1879), Bruges for 'The Morning of the Festival' (1880), Hamburg for 'An Old Hanse Town' (1880), Luneburg for 'An Old German Mill' (1880) and Wisby for 'Towing in the Prize' (1891). But to each composition Haig adds something of his own. His anthologies are held together by force of imagination. And there is no monotony of mood. 'A Quiet Hour': twilight peace; rising smoke and tapering spires; still water and restful shadows on a summer evening. 'The Morning of the Festival': movement; excitement; 'busy revellers in barges being rowed along a canal, usually smooth and always sluggish, but with its surface now rippling and quivering beneath the stroke of oars. Gaily dressed feasters ... waiting to join their friends in boats. ... [And, of course] above and beyond them Gothic buildings such as ... Haig ... always loved to draw'.[105]

Interior or exterior. In 'The Church of St Francis, Assisi' (1903), for instance, the sepulchral stillness inside the Lower Chapel is beautifully evoked: 'the gloom as of the grave, the arches bending heavily over the shrine, the scheme of decoration'.[106] Haig's view of the interior is certainly dramatic. But his vision of the exterior is sensational. 'Assisi, October Evening'
58 (1902) [182]: 'Evening glow and evening shadows. ... The church stands out white upon the summit of the hill, illumined by the rays of the setting sun. The wooded hillside below it and the town beyond ... are in shadow. Below, the river is running in flood. ... On the hither side two monks are walking together on the bank. ... Peacefulness and contrast of fading light and deep shadow – the restfulness of evening.'[107] No wonder, when Ruskin dreamed of escape, his preferred alternative retreats were 'a cell at Assisi or a shepherd's cottage in Cumberland'.[108]

If we measure Haig against his greatest contemporaries in the world of etching – Whistler, Haden and Zorn – he does not often compete. But they, and others like them – Keene, Strang, Watson, Herkomer and the Slocombes – were really competitors in a different field. Traditionally, English etchers – like the old

masters before them – produced prints for portfolios or for miniature frames in diminutive rooms. Haig produced 'pictures'. In effect, he transported a Continental tradition of large etched topography to an England still accustomed to small-scale portfolios. His prints were big: 'Pampeluna' (1887) [67] measures 47
more than a yard across. They were designed to be framed, hung, and viewed upon a wall – preferably in a library of oak and brass. Close to, their lines may seem a little heavy, almost crude. But at a distance their shapes can appear luminous, even haunting. Some of his full-scale compositions – 'The Vesper Bell', 'The Quiet Hour', 'The Morning of the Festival' – are by any standards extraordinarily accomplished. And even on a small scale his work can stand comparison with the very best of his rivals: his 'Cologne: Night Effect (1886)' [66] – dreamy, evocative, 46
technically superb – has as much economy of line as anything by Keene, and twice the pictorial impact. Haig's full-blown medieval fantasies did not set out to compete with Whistler's nocturnes. Their competitors were the mezzotints after Landseer, the line-engravings and photogravures after Frith, the French etchings after Burne-Jones, the English etchings after Fred Walker. Only Strang employed a similar scale, and he failed. Haig must have dominated the exhibitions of the Royal Society of Painter-Etchers just as Frith, Holman Hunt and Landseer once dominated the Royal Academy: by pictorial drama and sheer size. Not surprisingly, he was a regular prize-winner at international shows: Munich in 1890, Chicago and Berlin in 1891, Adelaide in 1887, and Paris in 1882, 1889 and 1900.

Etching certainly turned out to be something of a gold-mine for Haig. Occasionally his plates were published in the provinces: the 'Kirkstall Abbey' set (1892) [111–2, 121–2] were appropriately sold by R. Jackson of Leeds. But his usual agent was Robert Dunthorne of Vigo Street, London.[109] Dunthorne was an experienced, up-market operator, and most of Haig's plates sold quickly – especially in America. 'St Gilles, Arles' (1898) [78] grossed 5,000 guineas, and his six etchings of St Mark's (1897–9) [147, 151, 159–162] grossed little less than £10,000. Of course the artist received only a percentage of these sums. Even so, by the end of the 1880s Haig must certainly have been well off.[110] His other chief print-seller was the down-market firm of J. S. Virtue & Co. Virtue seems to have bought outright the copyright of the 'Old German Mill' (1880) and 'Old Hanse Town' (1883). Hence their republication, steel-faced, in the *Art Journal* (1881, 1883) and in Virtue's *Choice Examples of Modern Etchings* (1887) and *Gallery of Modern Etchings* (1890). Both publishers joined forces to market 'Cologne' (1891): first Dunthorne sold off 150 proofs; then Virtue published the plate broadcast in the *Art Journal* of 1892. Financially, the process must have been more or less comparable to that of modern book publishing: a title is often sold first of all in hardback, then disposed of soon afterwards under a paperback imprint. It must have been Virtue, however, who tempted Haig to cater directly for a mass audience. In 1887 he commissioned 'The Round Tower, Windsor' [70] for Queen Victoria's golden jubilee. And in 1900–1 the start of a new reign suggested 'Balmoral'[170], 'Buckingham Palace' [172], 'Linlithgow' [173], 'Windsor Castle' [165] and 'The Altar, Westminster Abbey' [178]. The result was artistically unfortunate. All five are hard, unsympathetic and poorly drawn. Many of Haig's later etchings are in fact mediocre. Still, they sold well.

In their heyday, some of Haig's larger works sold at five times their published price. Those 'tall, mysterious etchings of foreign towers and cathedrals', noted *The Artist* in 1892, 'are seldom seen in shop windows because printsellers rarely have copies for sale'.[111] When it appeared in 1879, 'The Vesper Bell' was published at five guineas; when a proof plate was auctioned at the Tom Taylor sale of 1881 it fetched sixteen guineas.[112] That was a plate which had always been rare: only fifty impressions were ever made. But, until the end of the century at least, Haig's etchings remained at a premium. Then the reaction set in. At his death in 1921, the obituaries were tepid in the extreme. 'An able and fertile artist in his particular line,' mused *The Times*; 'thirty years ago [he] would have been reckoned among the most popular etchers of his time.' His name had long been 'familiar to all who liked large, effective presentations of old cities, pinnacles and towers'. He 'obtained a multitude of gold medals and diplomas at foreign exhibitions. But he cannot be said to have ever commended himself to fastidious collectors'.[113]

True enough. But 'fastidious collectors' of etchings have oscillated over the years in their fondness for precision or imprecision of image. By the time of Haig's death, however, the preference for imprecision was very much in the ascendant. 'It is a paradoxical truth', explained one authority in 1912, 'that the more an etcher leaves out of his plate the more it is desired by the connoisseur. . . . One feels this as one looks over the learned and patiently elaborate architectural plates of Axel Haig; one wishes he had left out at least half of each, and given one's imagination some stimulus.'[114] In 1968, in a well publicised sale, five of his better etchings were knocked down at Christie's for a total of five guineas.[115] That was the nadir of Haig's reputation. Since then prices have risen substantially, and they continue to rise.

If an artist lives on, not only in his own work, but also in the work of his pupils, then Haig is unlikely to be wholly forgotten. Axel Tallberg (1860–1928) and A. M. Lindström (1894–) came under his spell. More important, it fell to Haig to train perhaps the greatest of modern etchers, his fellow countryman Anders Zorn (1860–1920).[116] In 1882 young Zorn settled temporarily in England and naturally went to Haig for advice. His very first etchings were in fact portraits of his new master. In all he produced three etched portraits of Haig, two in 1882, one in 1884. Haig instructed Zorn in the technique of etching – but there is no stylistic link. Zorn admired Rembrandt above all etchers, and his hazy chiaroscuro is worlds away from Haig's painstaking precision.[117] Even so, as a teacher – and as an artist in his own right – Haig can claim 'a position unique in the history of Swedish graphics'.[118] Etching rather than lithography remained his favourite medium. But at least two of his lithographs – 'Girl Winding Wool' [L3B] and 'Lady Reading by a Lamp' [L9] – have come to be accepted as classics.[119]

* * *

As an architect, Haig never made much of a name for himself. No doubt there were a number of unexecuted designs and one or two private commissions.[120] But on the whole Haig's architectural practice was limited to church restoration.

The lure of restoration – the desire to re-create the past in tangible form, and perhaps even to surpass it – was very much

part of the Victorian vision. Haig's evocative views of Uppsala
34, 39 Cathedral [32, 47], entitled 'Pictures of the Future', were in fact
intended as programmes for restoration – programmes never
taken up: the job went to Hugo Zettervall of Germany.[121] Haig
was, however, responsible for restorations and extensions
(1883–8) at Floda[122] in Södermanland [89–91], the setting for 'A
Swedish Pulpit' (1891) [33]; at Dalhem (1899–1904)[123] [149]
and at Ardré (1896–1902),[124] both on the isle of Gothland. All
three involved refurbishment of late medieval wall paintings, and
in this Haig was assisted by two of his friends, Almquist and
C. W. Petterson. In Gothland also he was responsible for the
external renovation of Wisby Cathedral (1896–1903),[125] in con-
junction with E. H. Dodgshun of Leeds.

As a restorer, Haig seems to have been less insensitive than most of his Swedish contemporaries. But he did reveal more than a streak of Romantic ruthlessness. At Dalhem, for example, his painted murals – 'medieval' tableaux, such as Ansgar preaching before Viking chiefs at Birka – make few concessions to their fourteenth-century neighbours.[126] In a way, of course, he was simply transposing into a different medium the compositional techniques of his fantasy etchings. In his etched interior of Amiens (1893) [118] he had no scruples about modelling the carving of one pillar on the altar of St Riquier near Abbeville. For Leon (1895) [139] he even introduced a non-existent roof. Such liberties in art – even in architecture – are all part of the eclectic game. In architectural restoration, however, the rules should be rather less lax.

Haig spent the bulk of his working life in London.[127] But after
1892 he retreated to Haslemere. Here he designed himself a
5 house (1891) [116], on part of an estate owned by one of
Burges's early patrons, H. G. Yatman of Ferndene. There he
spent the closing years of his life, the winters at least – 'an
amiable, smiling old man with a fine Viking beard'.[128] Summers
were still reserved for the family home in Gothland. And Swedish
subjects – St Catherine's church, for instance, towering above
49 Stockholm harbour [74] – remained a staple part of his artistic
output. From 1882 onwards he was an active member of the
Swedish Academy of Art in Stockholm. As late as 1905 he
published a lithograph of the 'Church at Gothen in the Island of

Gothland'.[129] And he remained very proud of his Swedish decorations: he was a Knight Commander of the Wasa, and a Knight of the Northern Star. Even so, in all but the legal sense, Haig had long before become a naturalised Briton, a 'proxy Englishman',[130] happiest in leafy Haslemere.

Haslemere, towards the end of the century, was by no means an aesthetic or intellectual desert. George Eliot wrote part of *Middlemarch* at Brookbank. Frederic Harrison spent his summers at Blackdown Cottage, and George Bernard Shaw arrived there in 1900. Sir Arthur Conan Doyle lived for some years at Undershaw, as did J. W. Whymper at The Town House in Haslemere High Street. Gerard Manley Hopkins died at The Garth in 1889. He is commemorated by a stained glass window in the parish church, along with one Haslemere resident whose connection was rather less fleeting, Alfred Lord Tennyson. Tennyson arrived at Aldworth in 1868, and stayed twenty-five years. James Knowles designed him a new house, a Victorian Camelot in Anglo-French Gothic, looking out – as Henry James put it – 'over one of the grandest sweeps of views in England'.[131] Gladstone was not the only famous visitor.

Haig exhibited regularly at the Haslemere Society of Artists. In fact he acted as its President from 1904 to 1920. The Haslemere Weaving Society and Guild of Handicraft, the Hammer Vale Pottery, the later Dolmetsch workshops – Haslemere might almost be described as a microcosm of the Arts and Crafts movement. Even the inn-sign of the semi-temperance Fox and Pelican was painted by Walter Crane. Up at Lythe Hill – a Tudoresque mansion of 1868 by F. P. Cockerell and George Aitchison – the squire of Haslemere, a banker-aesthete named James Stewart Hodgson, collected pictures by Rossetti, Holman Hunt, Richmond, Leighton and Stacy Marks.[132] Down in the village, the Working Men's Club and the Educational Museum still stand as evidence of a more practical philanthropy. Here Haig seems to have found his *métier*, embedded in stockbroker's Tudor, far from the Baltic Sea.

Haig's own house, Grayshurst [116], is still there, red-brick, 5
tile-hung, half-timbered, set high on a hill with panoramic views. Picture it in its heyday, the hall hung with Swedish tapestry and festooned with pictures. The drawing-room is 'so closely covered

with water-colours ... that an opinion as to the pattern of the wall-paper is almost a matter of guesswork'.[133] By the dining-room's deep-set chimney-piece hangs the 'Interior of Burgos'. And there are more etchings here too, their frames festooned with ivy which has wormed its way in through the windows. Upstairs there are etchings by Whistler and water-colours by many hands. And then there is the studio, opening into the hall, with rows of books at one end, hung with etchings and sketches, and strewn with the paraphernalia of the etcher's trade – 'there is none of the free space that is associated with a painter's studio'. Tables and chairs, even a miniature billiard-table, are piled high with sketch-books and papers. 'Open a carved oak cupboard – sketch-books again, not by dozens but by scores ... filled with notes ... scraps of landscapes ... sketches of buildings ... notes of detail ... studies of figures'. 'On the easel is whatever plate may be in the course of preparation, and beyond is another studio, or rather a workshop, with water-supply, baths for the immersion of plates, bottles of acid, a printing press, and all that is necessary to the etcher's craft. Pull out a drawer anywhere and it is full of proofs or of drawings. ... Truth to tell ... the studio is not altogether a tidy place.'[134]

Not far from Grayshurst stands the church of All Saints, Grayswood, built to Haig's designs in 1900–2. Paid for by another neighbour, A. H. Harman, its wooden bell-turret fits snugly into the Surrey landscape. But, inside, its timbered ceilings have more than a hint of Scandinavia. Here Haig was eventually buried – far from the cliffs of Gothland, but beneath a rock of craggy shape and a runic inscription of his own design.

Haig's last performance as an architect occurred in 1910. He supplied the design for London's Swedish Church in Harcourt Street, W.1. For years he had been a prominent member of the capital's Swedish community, in fact President of the Swedish Society in London.[135] D. B. Niven and H. H. Wigglesworth were called in as executant architects – after all, Haig was now over seventy years of age. Still, there is something about this church – a tall, high-shouldered vessel, butting its way through Marylebone – which conjures up memories of its author's Baltic homeland.

From Gothland to Haslemere: Haig's life-story is almost a

commentary on the decline of the Gothic Revival. The Victorian vision of the Middle Ages had many of the qualities and defects of his own etchings: omnivorous eclecticism, sentimentality, technical virtuosity, theatricality, selectivity, prolixity, obsession with detail, even a touch of the absurd. When Dr Conan Doyle threw a Christmas fancy dress ball at the Beacon Hotel, Hindhead, in 1898, Axel Herman Haig came dressed as a Viking.[136] In a letter[137] to Frank Short, accompanied by a photo- 2
graph, he jocularly explained his choice of garb:

> Herewith I send you, as promised, the portrait of a scoundrelly old sea-robber of my acquaintance. Unfortunately the sword is hidden, also the cloak-buckle, which is of fair workmanship, also a chain. The whole creature is too clean, but after he has been on some murderous expedition, no doubt he will acquire that special grimness, necessary for picturesque effect. . . . The portrait is not archaeologically correct and is not meant to be, only a fancy to meet the requirements of a certain occasion.

Like his etchings, Haig's fancy dress tells us at least as much about the Victorian era as it does about the Middle Ages.

Notes

The following abbreviations are used.

A	*The Architect*
AA	Architectural Association
B	*The Builder*
BA	*British Architect*
BN	*Building News*
E	*The Ecclesiologist*
PLU	Present Location Unknown
RA	Royal Academy
RE	Royal Society of Painter-Etchers & Engravers
RIBA	Royal Institute of British Architects

1 On the topography of nineteenth-century Gothland, see Murray's *Handbook for Travellers in Sweden* (1883), pp. 133–5; H. Marryatt, *One Year in Sweden: visit to Gothland*, 2 vols (1862); [R. Cotton] 'Silvanus', *Rambles in Sweden and Gothland* (1842); S. Laing, *Sweden*, (1839). For its churches, see A. Heales, *The Ecclesiology of Gothland* (1889); *Ecclesiologist*, VIII, N. S. V (1848), pp. 205–16, XIII, N. S. X (1852), p. 30 and XIX, N.S. XVI (1856), pp. 141–9, 205–10; *RIBA Journal*, N.S. II (1886), pp. 82–4; *Trans. St Paul's Eccles. Soc.*, II (1886–90), pp. 204–13; N. M. Mandelgren, *Monuments Scandinaves du Moyen Age* (Paris, 1862), reviewed *BN*, XX (1871), pp. 239–40, and *Notes sur l'exécution technique de nos vielles peintures d'église* (Stockholm, 1872).

2 There is no modern biography of Haig. Apart from periodicals and newspapers – and of course Haig's own drawings, watercolours and prints – the following texts formed the starting-point for this study: E. A. Armstrong, *Axel Herman Haig and his Work* (1905); *Svensk Konstnärs Lexikon*, III (1958), pp. 213–5; *Sale Catalogue of the Collection of J. Boland* (American Art Association, New York, 1919); *Sale Catalogue of the R. H. Hood Collection* (American Art Association, New York, 1919); A. Gauffin, 'A. H. Hägg', in *Hvar 8 dag* (1910), no. 13; E. G. Folcker, 'En etsning af A. H. Hägg', in *Ord och bild* (1897), pp. 191–2. For Haig's ancestry, see A. Kinberg, *Gothländska Slägter* (1839); E. Nyberg, *Gothlandsk Släktbok* (1938); B. Boethius, ed., *Svenskt Biografiskt Lexikon*, band XIX (1969).

3 E. Hägg, *Amiral Jacob Hägg (1839–1932) Hans liv och hans verk* (1934).

4 M. B. Adams, 'Architectural Drawings', *RIBA Journal*, N.S. I (1884–5),

pp. 111–8, 128. In discussion afterwards, Adams defended the English 'perspective' school; Phéné Spiers supported the 'beaux arts' tradition. Adams's paper carried on from W. Burges 'Architectural Drawing,' RIBA Papers (1860–61) 15–23. His list of exhibits (*RIBA Journal*, N.S. I, 1884–5, pp. 89–91) included John Dobson's 'Seaton Delaval' (1815): 'the first coloured drawing of a strictly architectural subject shown at the R.A.'; Burges's 'Sabrina Fountain' (lent by Pullan); Deshon's 'Senlis' (lent by Adams); one drawing by Haig (lent by Haig himself); and Allom's 'Seraglio Gardens' (lent by Mrs J. S. Storr).

5 For perspective artists – and techniques – see G. Stamp, *The Great Perspectivists* (1982).

6 RA, 1880, no. 1181; *Marble Halls*, no. 112 (India Office Library).

7 Haig was a member of the Canterbury Lodge (W. T. Pike, *Surrey at the Opening of the Twentieth Century*, Brighton, 1907, 176). For Burges's interest in Freemasonry and Rosicrucianism, see J. Mordaunt Crook, *William Burges and the High Victorian Dream* (1981), pp. 99–101.

8 'Interior, with court in session' (Victoria and Albert Museum, prints and drawings; W. Burges, *Report to the Courts of Justice Commission*, 1867, pl. 3; *The Strange Genius of William Burges, Art-Architect*, ed. J. Mordaunt Crook, 1981, no. A.12); 'Interior, great hall' (Victoria and Albert Museum, prints and drawings; Burges, *Report*, pl. 4; *W. Burges, Art-Architect*, no. A.13); 'Exterior, Strand View', *B.N.*, xiv (1867), p. 308. For details of the competition, see J. Mordaunt Crook, *William Burges and the High Victorian Dream* (1981), pp. 246–52.

9 RA, 1870, no. 781; *A.*, IV (1870), p. 7.

10 RA, 1870, nos 744, 752; *W. Burges, Art-Architect*, no. A.46.

11 For details, see *W. Burges and the High Victorian Dream*, pp. 245–6.

12 RIBA, Arc. IV, ii, 5; RA, 1872, no. 1210; *W. Burges, Art-Architect*, no. A.92.

13 RA, 1872, no. 1217.

14 RIBA, Arc. IV, i; RA, 1872, no. 1242; *W. Burges, Art-Architect*, no. C.31.

15 A. R. Willard, 'The Development of College Architecture in America', *New England Magazine*, XVI (1899), pp. 524–6.

16 Worcester College archives; *W. Burges, Art-Architect*, no. A.14.

17 RA, 1865, no. 785; sold, Abbot & Holder Ltd, 1980. PLU.

18 RA, 1873, nos 1133 and 1148; *A.*, XXVII (1882), p. 251; *W. Burges, Art-Architect*, no. C.29.

19 RA, 1874, no. 1146; *W. Burges, Art-Architect*, no. A.43.

20 RA nos 952 (Dome), 995 (Chancel) and 1005 (General View); *W. Burges, Art-Architect*, no. C.32 (Chancel). For details, see J. Mordaunt Crook, 'William Burges and the Completion of St Paul's', *Antiquaries Journal*, LXII (2), (1981).

21 *A.*, XIX (1878), p. 270.

22 RIBA, Arc. IV, vi, 1; *A.* XXVII (1882), p. 251; *W. Burges, Art-Architect*, no. C.27.

23 RA, 1880, no. 1178; *W. Burges, Art-Architect*, no. A.103. Just a year before, Haig also published a lithograph of Lord Bute's study 'A Room in Cardiff Castle' (*A*. XXII, 1879, p. 89).
24 E. W. Godwin called it 'the architectural drawing *par excellence* of our time' (*BA*, XXIII, 1885, p. 61).
25 'The whole drawing looks like a woodcut ... from the Nuremburg Chronicle' (*E*, XXIII, N.S. XX, 1862, p. 163).
26 *AA Notes*, V (1891), p. 51.
27 R. Blomfield, *Architectural Drawing and Draughtsmanship* (1912), p. 90.
28 *Church Builder* (1875), pp. 86–8. For an example, see 'Proposed Design, Middle Temple Hall' (n.d.), RIBA, W1/49.
29 *BN*, XV (1868), p. 705.
30 *ex inf.* Paul Joyce.
31 *BN*, XV (1868), p. 655.
32 *BN*, XVI (1869), p. 54.
33 *BN*, XVI (1869), pp. 158, 577.
34 *BN*, XVII (1869), p. 392.
35 *BN*, XIX (1870), p. 189.
36 *AA Notes*, V. (1891), p. 51.
37 *BA*, XXIII (1885), p. 61.
38 *AA Notes*, V (1891), pp. 50–1.
39 RA, 1870, no. 738.
40 RA, 1871, no. 974.
41 'View in Limburg on the Lahn' (RA, 1874, no. 843); 'View from the street of Tombs, Pompeii' (RA, 1876, no. 666); 'An old Courtyard, Nuremburg' (RA, 1876, no. 736); 'In a garden at Palermo' (RA, 1876, no. 776); 'Pulpit in the church of San Fermo Maggiore, Verona' (RA, 1877, no. 1214); 'At Loches, Touraine – night in autumn' (RA, 1879, no. 848).
42 *A*, XIX (1878), pp. 8, 29–30, 112; and LXXII (1905), pp. 13, 32.
43 For example 'A Street in Nuremburg' and 'The Castle of Nuremburg' (*A*, xvii, 1877, pp. 8, 42 and LXXIII, 1905, p. 96).
44 *A*, XIX (1878), p. 50, and LXXIII (1905), p. 65.
45 *A*, XIX (1878), p. 208, and LXXIII (1905), p. 65.
46 *A*, XXI (1879), pp. 97, 113, and LXXIII (1905), p. 48.
47 *A*, XXI (1879), p. 129, and LXXIII (1905), p. 32.
48 *A*, XXI (1879), pp. 7, 11, and LXXIII (1905), p. 176.
49 *A*, XXI (1879), p. 35, and LXXIII (1905), p. 160.
50 *A*, XXI (1879), p. 53.
51 *A*, XXI (1879), p. 175, and LXXIII (1905), p. 112; *A*, XXIII (1880), p. 9, and LXXIII (1905), p. 128.
52 *A*, XXV (1881), p. 11.
53 ibid.
54 Armstrong, *Haig*, pp. 66–9.
55 Mostly brick details from Spain and north Italy. Dedicated to Sir Gilbert Scott.

56 RA, 1880, no. 1253.
57 RA, 1881, no. 1181.
58 RA, 1882, no. 1255.
59 A photographic reproduction of this print was published in Vienna; a copy is in the Museum of Fine Arts, Boston.
60 'A street in Vitré, Brittany' (RA, 1882, no. 1065); 'A street in Seville with "La Giralda"' (RA, 1884, no. 1457); 'Seville Cathedral, Puerta de San Roque' (RA, 1884, no. 1464); 'Moorish Archway, Toledo' (RA, 1885, no. 1599); 'The Cathedral of Uppsala, Sweden' (RA, 1885, no. 1614); 'Westminster Abbey' (RA, 1885, no. 1644); 'The Alhambra from the Generalife' (RA, 1886, no. 1245); 'The Magdalen, Oxford' (RA, 1886, no. 1428); 'From St Edmund's Chapel, Westminster Abbey' (RA, 1886, no. 1468); 'Alcazar, Segovia' (RA, 1887, no. 1462); 'The Cathedral of St George, Limburg-on-the-Lahn' (RA, 1887, no. 1482); 'The Basilica of St Gilles, near Arles' (RA, 1888, no. 1638); 'Evening, Cairo' (RA, 1892, no. 1259); 'On the Arlanzon, near Burgos' (RA, 1894, no. 1491). He also exhibited regularly at the Dudley Gallery, both in watercolour and in black and white, his prices rising from 10 guineas to 50 guineas between 1869 and 1876. After 1883, when the Dudley Gallery ceased to show non-member watercolours, he used the Royal Institute of Painters in Watercolour. He also exhibited at the Royal Institute of Fine Arts, Glasgow and at the Walker Art Gallery, Liverpool.
61 *Works*, XIX, pp. 90–2, 100–1.
62 *Works*, XIX, p. 112.
63 Sir F. Newbolt, *History of the Royal Society of Painter-Etchers and Engravers* (1930); T. Simpson, *Modern Etchings*(1919).
64 See F. Wedmore, in *English Etchings*, pt LXXV (1885–9), pp. 29–30.
65 *Magazine of Art*, I (1878), pp. 146–8, 217–20.
66 H. R. Robertson, in *English Etchings*, pt LXI (1885–9), p. 1.
67 Armstrong, *Haig*, p. 56.
68 *BN*, LXXXVII (1904), p. 608. Previous one-man exhibitions of Haig's work were held at Dunthorne's Rembrandt's Head Gallery in 1883 (sketches) and at J. W. Vokins's Gallery in 1887 (prints).
69 *The Artist*, 2 July 1883, p. 217.
70 Obituary, *Art Journal*, 1880, p. 248; *B*, XXXIX (1880), pp. 105, 119.
71 *The Times*, 3 April 1880, pp. 5–6.
72 *The Etcher*, July 1880.
73 *The Etcher*, April 1880; RA, 1880, no. 1253.
74 *The Etcher*, 1879, pl. 16.
75 *Art Journal*, 1881, pp. 32, 62.
76 *Art Journal*, 1883, p. 144.
77 *Art Journal*, 1892, pp. 2–4.
78 *BN*, LXXXVII (1904), p. 608.
79 *A*, XXI (1879), p. 63, and LXXIII (1905), p. 112.
80 *The Times*, 22 March 1882, p. 4.
81 *Art Journal*, 1892, pp. 2–4.

82 *B*, LII (1887), p. 340.
83 *Athenaeum*, 1882, p. 250.
84 *Art Journal*, 1882, p. 126.
85 Armstrong, *Haig*, pp. 81–2, 85–6.
86 *Modern Painters*, III (1856); *Works*, ed. Cook and Wedderburn, V, pp. 252–3.
87 This slim volume contained reproductions of seven etchings. See the Chronological List, nos 51–3, 58–61.
88 Armstrong, *Haig*, pp. 48–50.
89 *Works*, XXXIII, p. 353.
90 *Works*, XIX, p. 114.
91 *Works*, XXXVII, p. 445; XIV, pp. 336–7.
92 *Works*, XIV, p. 337.
93 *The Portfolio*, V (1874), pp. 25–9.
94 *Works*, XX, pp. 124–5.
95 *The Artist*, 1890, p. 215.
96 *The Artist*, 1898, p. 238.
97 *RIBA Journal*, 3rd series, XXVIII (1921), p. 582.
98 *Svensk Konstnärs Lexikon*, iii (1958), pp. 213–5.
99 'St Étienne Le Vieux, Caen' (*A*, LXXIII, 1905, p. 144); 'Old Farm Buildings at Saint-German De Livet, Calvados' (*A*, LXXIII, 1905, p. 208).
100 Exhibited RE 1918, no. 82, 83.
101 Armstrong, *Haig*, pp. 58–9.
102 ibid., p. 168.
103 *Works*, V, p. 253.
104 'The Ethics of the Sketch-Book', *RIBA Journal*, 3rd series, III (1895–6), pp. 489–91.
105 Armstrong, *Haig*, p. 35.
106 ibid., p. 156.
107 ibid., pp. 153–4.
108 *Fors Clavigera*: *Works*, ed., Cook and Wedderburn, XXVIII, p. 485.
109 Dunthorne's Rembrandt's Head Gallery in Vigo Street was next door to John Lane's Bodley Head.
110 When he died in 1921, at 26 Kent Road, Southsea, Sussex, he left only £2,312 4s 2d in the UK. In Sweden there may have been much more: he had managed to purchase the family estate in 1887, and sold it to his brother in 1917. Mrs Haig died at 5 Giltar Terrace, Penally, Pembrokeshire, on 14 February 1930, leaving £3,513 7s 5d (Probate Records, Somerset House). Haig presented many of his trial proofs to the British Museum in 1903; more were presented by Mrs Haig in 1922.
111 *The Artist*, 1892, p. 59.
112 Armstrong, *Haig*, p. 32.
113 *The Times*, 27 August 1921, p. 11.
114 M. C. Salaman, *Whitman's Print-Collector's Handbook* (1912), p. 69.

115 18 July 1968, lot 349: 'Seville' (1883), 'Toledo' (1889), 'Burgos' (1887), 'Amiens' (1893), 'St Mark's' (1897).

116 Other followers included Ferdinand Boberg, Carl Möller, Ludwig Peterson, Gustav Clason, Hjalmar Molin, Karl Flodman and Robert Haglund. See G. Nordensvan, *Svensk Konst och Svenska Konstnärer*, (1925).

117 K. Asplund, *Anders Zorn* (1921), pp. 16, 61, 72. Together with Zorn and A. M. Lindström, Haig was involved in 1885 in a dispute with the Swedish Academy of Art about teaching methods.

118 *Svensk Konstnärs Lexikon*, loc cit.

119 ibid.

120 For example 'Design for a Half-Timbered House' (1873), RIBA Drawings Collection, W1/3a–b.

121 Armstrong, *Haig*, p. 79; B. G. Söderberg, *Svensk Kyrko Mälningar* (1951).

122 Haig drawings, Swedish National Archives, Stockholm, and Ministry of Education, resolution of King in Council, 21 December 1883, no. 20; Söderberg, op. cit., p. 27, ill.

123 Haig drawings, Swedish National Archives, Stockholm, and Ministry of Education, resolution of King in Council, 28 April 1899, no. 8; *Sveriges Kyrkor, Konst historikst inventarium*, Gothland 4: 1, pp. 151–217. See also C. Lindgren, in *Ord och bild*, V (1897); Söderberg, op. cit., 28, ill.

124 Haig drawings, Swedish National Archives, Stockholm, and Ministry of Education, resolution of King in Council, 21 May 1897, no. 8; *Sveriges Kyrkor, Konsthistorikst inventarium*, Gothland 4: 2, pp. 775–840.

125 Haig drawings, Swedish National Archives, Stockholm, and Ministry of Education, resolution of King in Council, 25 November 1898, no. 3; *Sveriges Kyrkor Konsthistorikst inventarium*, no. 175; Armstrong, *Haig*, p. 63.

126 Söderberg, op. cit., passim.

127 William Burges's Estimate and Address Book (Victoria and Albert Museum MSS) lists four addresses in succession: 56 Erdley Crescent, Warwick Road, West Brompton; 236 Marylebone Road; Rose Cottage, Trinity Street, Ryde, Isle of Wight; 32 Randolph Gardens, Kilburn, N.W. Haig's London Club was the Savage.

128 K. Asplund, *Anders Zorn* (1921), p. 16.

129 *A*, LXXIII (1905), p. 192.

130 E. G. Folcker, in *Ord och bild* (1897), pp. 191–2.

131 Priscilla Metcalf, *James Knowles* (Oxford, 1980), pp. 198–208.

132 E. W. Swanton, *Bygone Haslemere* (1914), pp. 272–4.

133 Armstrong, *Haig*, p. 61.

134 ibid., pp. 62–3.

135 E. Sjöstrand, *Märkliga Svenskar i England* (1923).

136 'Haslemere Notes, 1870–1900' (Haslemere Educational Museum), f. 106.

137 17 March 1900 (in the collection of Michael Darby).

Chronological list of prints

All known etchings are included, arranged in chronological order, by year. Except for the first year, when Haig numbered his prints, no attempt has been made to place them in a more precise order; series, however, have usually been kept together. Where possible, all items have been measured – height before width – but some measurements have necessarily been taken from Armstrong or from the Hood and Boland sale catalogues. These are marked (A), (H), and (B) respectively. Measurements vary considerably from impression to impression: only major differences, therefore, have been noted.

Where known, price and limitation is recorded immediately after the title or description. Most of these were published by Dunthorne and many, after 1894, have his publication line (marked *) or stamp on them. Limitation applied only to published 'proofs'; trial proofs and presentation prints are probably excluded, as are prints with letters. No attempt has been made to differentiate between states except where lettered impressions are known. Many trial proofs, for example, are in the British Museum, presented by Haig in 1903 or by his widow in 1922.

All prints are etchings unless otherwise described, with the addition of an acid tone or thin uniform aquatint ground, after 1880. Almost all prints have Haig's monogram and date in a lower corner; many are inscribed in the image. A few are signed in full and five of the first six are numbered.

There are probably a number of other prints in existence. Some early etchings are known from one impression (No. 17) or from sale catalogues. Haig's titles often vary. His 150 exhibits at the Royal Society of Painter-Etchers and Engravers often bear titles different from the surviving prints. Only where the title does not correspond with a known or described print are these recorded, under the year of their exhibition.

1877

1 **A Windmill**
Some aquatint. 150 mm x 97 mm (B). A mill near Bruges that reminded Haig of one near Katthammarsvik.

2 **Waggon at Bruges**
Drypoint, 67 mm x 105 mm (H). Numbered No. 1.

3 **Verona – Women Washing Clothes**
95 mm x 130 mm (A). Aquatint added later.

4 **Nuremberg: A Courtyard**
223 mm x 140 mm (A).

5 **Unknown.**

6 **Rouen: St Ouen – A Cavalcade**
250 mm x 179 mm. The 'Cavalcade Rouen' exhibited, RE No. 96, 1906 and at Haslemere and listed in Dunthorne's catalogues of 1908 to 1913, with 150 proofs at 3 guineas. This print is dated 1890 in manuscript among otherwise accurate marginalia in a catalogue *c.* 1910 in the Victoria and Albert Museum. The only impression seen is on old paper. Misdated 1879 by Hood.

7 **Linlithgow – Three Figures in a Boat**
105 mm x 130 mm (A).

West Doorway, Holyrood
See No. 12.

8 **Holyrood, South Aisle** (50, 1½ guineas)
With slight aquatint. 256 mm x 182 mm. For Anderson's book.

9 **Linlithgow: East Side of Court** (150, 1½ guineas)
273 mm x 191 mm (A). For Anderson's book. The 150 proofs were not published till later, first appearing in Dunthorne's 1891 catalogue. This explains the large issue.

10 **Linlithgow – Dog, Man and Boy by a Barred Window**
251 mm x 165 mm (B). Probably for Anderson's book.

11 **Venice: View on a Canal**
102 mm x 147 mm (A). Date uncertain. Possibly more than one state.

1878

12 **West Doorway, Holyrood** (50, 1½ guineas)
279 mm x 204 mm. For Anderson's book. Some impressions have the title etched below. Misdated 1877 by Armstrong.

13 **Broughton Malherbe Church**
167 mm x 203 mm (H). Possibly a book illustration.

14 **Going His Rounds** (100, 1 guinea)
76 mm x 197 mm (A). A priest at Bruges.

15 **Ryde Harbour**
98 mm x 151 mm (H).

16 **Melrose: A View from the Chancel**
273 mm x 191 mm (A). For Anderson's book but probably never published.

17 **A Well at Verona**
270 mm x 178 mm.

1879

18 **The Vesper Bell** (50, 5 guineas)
553 mm x 324 mm. Based on Nuremburg. Trial proofs exist. Some proofs have a remarque. Originally published at 4 guineas.

19 **Verona: Ponte S. Pietro**
127 mm x 202 mm. Possibly the print of Verona published by Dunthorne between 1904 and 1908.

20 **Caen: Tower of St Pierre** (100, 2 guineas)
371 mm x 182 mm. Various states.
Rouen: St Ouen
See No. 6.

21 **Jedburgh Abbey: South Doorway** (50, 2 guineas)
255 mm x 202 mm. For Anderson's book.

22 **Flemish Lace Workers** (100, 1 guinea)
191 mm x 280 mm. At Bruges.

23 **A Corner at Huy** (25, 1½ guineas)
276 mm x 185 mm. Published in the *Etcher* with the addition of the artist's name etched on the plate.

1880

24 **The Morning of the Festival** (100, 5 guineas)
538 mm x 327 mm. Based on notes from Bruges. Trial proofs exist.

25 **A Quiet Hour** (100, 5 guineas)
540 mm x 323 mm. Based on Chartres.

26 **An Old German Mill** (100)
257 mm x 176 mm. The 100 signed proofs predate its appearance in the *Art Journal* and other publications. Based on Luneburg. Trial proofs exist.

27 **A Street in France** (200, 1 guinea)
181 mm x 121 mm (A). Inspired by Chartres.

28 **At Haddon Hall**
261 mm x 179 mm. The Elopement of Dorothy Vernon(?).

1881

29 **Chartres Cathedral: The Great North Porch** (250, 5 guineas)
576 mm x 431 mm. With a remarque of Haig sketching in the lower margin.

30 **Chartres Cathedral: In the Aisles** (250, 5 guineas)
353 mm x 508 mm. Trial proofs exist.

31 **Chartres brochure** (a) Title: Four saints
90 mm x 72 mm.
(b) Tailpiece: Lady on a shield
Tondo, 49 mm diameter.

32 **Uppsala: Design for the Restoration of the Cathedral** (100)
568 mm x 352 mm. Impressions with Swedish letters exist, some with tone worn off.

33 **A Swedish Pulpit – or – An Old Swedish Church**
253 mm x 176 mm. Floda before Haig's restoration. In early impressions the pastor has no skull-cap.

34 **Verona: Pulpit of San Fermo Maggiore** (250, 4 guineas)
453 mm x 311 mm. Some later impressions have a remarque of three angels singing. Etched for the American market but with 250 proofs for England. Armstrong, Hood, and Boland give the height as 14 inches (356 mm), but this must be an error.

1882

35 **Mont St Michel** (500, 10 guineas)
876 mm x 628 mm.
Mont St Michel: The Hawker
See No. 277.

36 **Chartres Cathedral: Under The Great North Porch** (250, 5 guineas)
578 mm x 436 mm.

37 **Chartres: Street Scene and Cathedral** (250, 5 guineas)
572 mm x 351 mm. From a viewpoint unobtainable even when the etching was made. Misdated 1889 by Boland.

38 **Charles Darwin's Study at Down, Near Orpington** (250, 3 guineas)
254 mm x 357 mm (A).

39 **Mont St Michel**
128 mm x 87 mm. A reduced version, dated 1882, of No. 35, made for the brochure. Signed proofs also exist.

40 **Mont St Michel brochure**
(a) Title: St Michael Overcoming the Dragon 123 mm x 83 mm.
(b) Tailpiece: The Dragon Eating Grapes.
Tondo, 82 mm diameter.

1883

41 **A Street in Seville** (300, 3 guineas)
703 mm x 356 mm.

42 **Peterborough Cathedral** (300, 5 guineas)
567 mm x 425 mm.

43 **River Scene, Spire over Trees**
184 mm x 286 mm. Possibly 'River Scene, Sweden – A punt and Figures on the Bank', in the Hood Sale as published in an uncertain edition with Dunthorne's stamp, probably 200 proofs at 1 guinea.

44 **A Swedish River – Sailing Boats and a Barge**
181 mm x 286 mm (A). Near Orebro.

45 **An Old Hanse Town** (150, 1½ guineas)
260 mm x 177 mm. Based on Hamburg. The 150 signed proofs predate its appearance in the *Art Journal* and other publications.

1884

46 **A Corner of Seville Cathedral** (300, 5 guineas)
702 mm x 353 mm.

47 **Uppsala Cathedral: Design for the Completion of the Interior** (100, 5 guineas, 1st state)
567 mm x 352 mm. Unlimited impressions were printed with Swedish letters in the lower margin at 3 guineas, apparently for a Swedish art union.

48 **Moorish Archway, Toledo** (300, 2 guineas)
364 mm x 213 mm. Some impressions have Dunthorne's stamp.

49 **In Toledo – The Cathedral** (150, 1 guinea)
Drypoint, 232 mm x 130 mm (A).

50 **Head of a Girl in Spanish Dress: Mrs Haig**
193 mm x 127 mm. An unfinished and unsigned proof in the British Museum is 158 mm wide.

1885

51 **Westminster Abbey: View from St Edmund's Chapel** (500, 5 guineas)
651 mm x 403 mm.

52 **Westminster Abbey: North Chancel Aisle** (500, 5 guineas)
597 mm x 400 mm.

53 **Westminster Abbey: View of the Chancel** (500, 2 guineas)
211 mm x 282 mm.

54 **The Fountain of St George** (100, 5 guineas)
485 mm x 318 mm. Based on the fountain at Rothenburg-ob-der-Tauber, Bavaria. Trial proofs exist.

55 **Winter, Orebro, Sweden**
130 mm x 79 mm (H).

56 **Waiting for the Ferry, Lubeck** (250, 1½ guineas)
353 mm x 206 mm (A).

57 **Plaza de la Constitucion, Seville**
232 mm x 143 mm (A). Aquatint added 1901.

1886

58 **Westminster Abbey: A Dark Corner** (500, 2 guineas)
325 mm x 188 mm.

59 **Westminster Abbey: The Poets' Corner** (500, 2 guineas)
304 mm x 187 mm.

60 **Westminster Abbey: Entrance to the Poets' Corner** (500, 2 guineas)
286 mm x 178 mm.

61 **Westminster Abbey: The Cloisters** (500, 2 guineas)
203 mm x 247 mm.

62 **Limburg on the Lahn** (650, 10 guineas)
878 mm x 626 mm. Etched as a pair to 'Mont St Michel', No. 35. Trial proofs exist.

63 **The Alcazar, Segovia**
623 mm x 404 mm.

64 **Magdalen College, Oxford** (500, 8 guineas)
475 mm x 328 mm.

Segovia: a street scene
See No. 223.

65 **Schloss Zwingenburg, on the Neckar** (250, 3 guineas)
400 mm x 262 mm. Misdated by Boland to 1887.

66 **Cologne, Night Effect** (100, 1½ guineas)
With aquatint, 157 mm x 203 mm. The plate was damaged and repaired during printing. Trial proofs exist.

1887

67 **Pampeluna, Returning from the Fair** (700, 12 guineas)
650 mm x 934 mm. Trial proofs exist.

68 **L'Église des Dominicains, Arles** (300, 4 guineas)
507 mm x 302 mm.

69 **On the Regent's Canal** (150, 5 guineas)
203 mm x 267 mm (A). Haig lived in Kilburn till 1892.

70 **Windsor Castle: The Round Tower** (150, 1½ guineas)
260 mm x 177 mm. 150 signed proofs with Dunthorne's publication line were taken but the plate was etched expressly for the *Art Journal* jubilee number, 1887.

71 **Washerwomen at Chartres – or – Washing Day, Chartres** (400, 1 guinea)
457 mm x 182 mm. Presented to subscribers to the Artists Benevolent Fund.

Schloss Zwingenburg
See No. 65.

72 **Wisby: Entrance to the Cathedral Yard**
245 mm x 172 mm. Two states: before and with Swedish letters.

1888

73 **Wisby: Two Sailing Boats**
468 mm x 660 mm (B).

74 **Stockholm: The Floating Market** (300? 5 guineas)
604 mm x 398 mm.

75 **A Hill Town in Navarre** (200, 3 guineas)
Aquatint and Line, 454 mm x 307 mm.

76 **In Church – Four Worshippers** (100, 1 guinea)
Aquatint, 197 mm x 153 mm (A). Possibly 'At Matins', at the RE in 1889 but 'In Church' was exhibited there in 1898.

77 **On The Swedish Coast – Sailing Vessels Near a Quay**
Aquatint, 130 mm x 181 mm (A).

78 **The Basilica of St Gilles, Arles** (625, 8 guineas)
727 mm x 500 mm. Trial proofs exist. Misdated by Armstrong to 1898.

79 **Stockholm – The Dome Silhouetted in Grey Heat-haze**
216 mm x 381 mm (H). Aquatint added in 1904.

1889

80 **Burgos: Interior – St Christopher over the Iron Screen** (500, 8 guineas)
688 mm x 452 mm.

81 **Toledo Cathedral: Interior – The Choir Passing under the Screen** (350, 8 guineas)
Aquatint, 677 mm x 456 mm.

82 **Cuenca – From across the Valley**
296 mm x 454 mm. 150 impressions of this or possibly of No. 84 were published by Dunthorne at 3 guineas.

83 **Cuenca: The Two Bridges**
461 mm x 333 mm.

84 **A Street in Cuenca**
454 mm x 295 mm.

85 **Grim Toledo – A Street** (100, 3 guineas)
Aquatint and line 279 mm x 308 mm (A). 483 mm x 308 mm (H and B).

86 **A Spaniard**
108 mm x 61 mm (H).

87 **Barcelona: Santa Maria del Mar** (150, 3 guineas)
482 mm x 310 mm. An impression with the publication line of W. R. Howell, Leeds, 1913, exists.

88 **Wisby: Morning – or – The Walk by the Shore**
With aquatint, 317 mm x 203 mm.

89 **Floda – The Church Seen over Fields from the Stream**
254 mm x 154 mm.

90 **Floda – The Church Seen across Trees**
226 mm x 149 mm.

91 **Floda – A Road Winding up to the Church**
Drypoint, 159 mm x 197 mm.
Chartres
See No. 37.
92 **In the Pyrenees**
216 mm x 140 mm (A). Near Argelès.
93 **Trafalgar Square**
238 mm x 153 mm (A).

1890

94 **Burgos Cathedral: Exterior** (400, 7 guineas)
696 mm x 456 mm.
95 **Cairo: Arab Students** (250, 8 guineas)
424 mm x 609 mm.
96 **Lubeck: The Sailors' Guild** (125, 5 guineas)
456 mm x 305 mm (A). Also called 'The Skippers' Guild'.
97 **Entrance to the Mosque of Mohammed Bey, Cairo** (200, 2 guineas)
388 mm x 258 mm.
98 **Cairo – Street Scene with a Merchant's Stall**
398 mm x 260 (A).
99 **In the Rhineland**
298 mm x 153 mm (A). Based on Coblenz.
100 **Fellahah, Cairo**
143 mm x 94 mm. Aquatint added 1901.

1891

101 **Segovia, Spain – The Cathedral High on the Left**
Originally 629 mm x 867 mm (A). Probably 'The Old Castilian City', RE, 1892, No. 235. Then cut in two:
101a **The Cathedral Hill**
629 mm x 422 mm (A).
101b **The Sierra Guadarrama in the Distance**
298 mm x 439 mm (A).
102 **In the Arab Quarter, Cairo** (275, 8 guineas)
614 mm x 408 mm.
103 **Vespers** (500, 5 guineas)
449 mm x 297 mm. Motifs from Beauvais.
104 **Wisby: Towing in the Prize,** AD 1500 (150, 2 guineas)
280 mm x 204 mm.
105 **Cologne: A Street Scene – or – Santa Maria in Capitol**
260 mm x 177 mm (A). A composition rather than a topographical view. 150 signed proofs were issued at 1½ guineas before publication in the *Art Journal* of 1892.

106 **Goslar – The Kaiserworth on the Right**
556 mm x 234 mm (A).

107 **Stockholm, Morning – St Catherine's from the Harbour** (100, 1 guinea)
Drypoint, 149 mm x 156 mm (A). 142 mm x 225 mm (H and B). There were two impressions, in different states, in the Hood sale.

108 **Stockholm Harbour – The Quays, Six Ships Tied Up to the Point**
With light aquatint, 156 mm x 235 mm.

109 **The Flying Dutchman**
RE, 1891, No. 207.
Possibly No. 279.

1892

110 **The Portals of Rheims Cathedral** (325, 8 guineas)
626 mm x 455 mm.

111 **Kirkstall Abbey – From the South East**
647 mm x 457 mm. This and Nos 112, 121 and 122 were published by R. Jackson, Commercial Street, Leeds.

112 **Kirkstall Abbey – Remains of the Tower**
391 mm x 256 mm.

113 **Castle Nowhere**
Aquatint, 156 mm x 200 mm (A). Possibly 'Stronghold', RE 1899, No. 43.

114 **Stockholm – Tug at Dawn**
Aquatint with some etching, 190 mm x 293 mm.

115 **Stockholm, the Harbour – Steam Tug Towing a Barge**
193 mm x 286 mm. Two states: before and with aquatint.

116 **Grayshurst, Haslemere – A Christmas Card**
83 mm x 118 mm. The print in the Hood and Boland sales whose measurements are given as $2\frac{1}{8}$ x $4\frac{3}{4}$ inches (154 mm x 121 mm) may possibly be a different plate.

117 **Quiet Corner, Cairo**
RE 1892, No. 115. Haig exhibited his four other Cairo views in 1891.

1893

118 **Amiens Cathedral: Interior** (450, 8 guineas)
692 mm x 467 mm. Trial proofs exist.

119 **Durham Cathedral** (425, 8 guineas)
626 mm x 438 mm.

120 **Goslar – The Kaiserworth on the Left** (150, 5 guineas)
526 mm x 274 mm. Boland misdated this 1895.

121 **Kirkstall Abbey: The Cloisters**
257 mm x 392 mm.

122 **Kirkstall Abbey: The Chapter House**
253 mm x 386 mm.

123 **Rheims Cathedral: North Transept** (150, 2½ guineas)
381 mm x 254 mm (A). Dated 1895 by Boland.

124 **English Pastoral**
260 mm x 372 mm (A). Said both to be near Kirkstall Abbey and near Haddon Hall.

125 **On the Swedish Coast – or – The Cavalcade**
157 mm x 235 mm. A composition near Marstrand. With heavy acid-tone.

126 **Hang It – A Georgian Picture Hanger**
89 mm square (A). Dated 1793, etched to fill a gap at the RE exhibition of 1893.

127 **Longitude – A Man Displaying a Picture of a Sunset**
83 mm x 44 mm. Also a gap filler at the RE.

128 **What Cheer? A Christmas Card**
132 mm x 92 mm.

1894

129 **Canterbury from the Stour** (250, 6 guineas)
412 mm x 611 mm (A). Proofs before publication line exist.

130 **Canterbury: The Pilgrims' Aisle*** (250, 4 guineas)
454 mm x 321 mm (A). Proofs before publication line exist.

131 **Canterbury Cathedral: Ruined Refectory in Front*** (250, 4 guineas)
459 mm x 325 mm. Proofs before publication line exist.

132 **On the Somme at Amiens**
190 mm x 207 mm. Similar to No. 169 i/ii.

133 **Toledo: The Conventual Church of San Juan de los Reyes** (150, 5 guineas)
438 mm x 303 mm.

Stockholm Harbour
See No. 114.

134 **On the Arlanzon, Near Burgos** (100, 1 guinea)
Aquatint, 157 mm x 232 mm.

135 **On a Swedish Lake** (100, 1 guinea)
Aquatint, 248 mm x 141 mm (A).

135a **St. Luke and the Sparrow**
9⅞" x 6⅞"

136 **The Legend of the Bells – A Christmas Card**
153 mm x 98 mm.

1895

Goslar
See No. 120.

Rheims
See No. 123.

137 **Tarragona Cathedral*** (250, 7 guineas)
594 mm x 393 mm.

138 **Palencia: The Altar of the Visitation*** (250, 7 guineas)
422 mm x 562 mm. Proofs before publication line exist.

139 **Leon – From the North East**
307 mm x 421 mm (A). Not topographically accurate. Probably 'Evening Motif From Leon'. RE, 1896, No. 123.

140 **Gothem, Gotland, Sweden**
406 mm x 298 mm (A).

141 **The Legend of the Bells** (150? 8 guineas)
613 mm x 423 mm. Trial and Cancelled proofs exist. A cut (382 mm x 244 mm) impression with inscription on the mount has been seen and is illustrated. 57

142 **Ascotia, Basque Provinces**
RE, 1895, No. 36, probably very small. See also No. 156.

1896

143 **Palencia: The Trascoro*** (250, 7 guineas)
604 mm x 401 mm.

144 **Burgos: View from the South – or – Burgos from the River** (150, 3 guineas)
Drypoint, 240 mm x 393 mm.

145 **Lichfield** (150, 2 guineas)
319 mm x 207 mm.

146 (a) **The Adoration of the Shepherds: A Christmas Card**
81 mm x 121 mm.
(b) **Grayshurst**
57 mm x 96 mm.
Two on one card.

Burgos: North Porch
RE, 1896, No. 24. See No. 179.

1897

147 **St Mark's, Venice: Interior*** (350, 7 guineas)
623 mm x 436 mm. Proofs before publication line exist.

148 **In the Aisles: Amiens Cathedral*** (250, 4 guineas)
278 mm x 369 mm. Proofs before publication line appear to exist.

149 **Dalhem, Gotland, Sweden**
272 mm x 346 mm (A).

150 **On Lake Mälaren, Stockholm**
RE, 1897, No. 107.

1898

Burgos Cathedral: North Porch
See No. 179.
St Gilles, Arles
See No. 78.

151 **St Mark's Venice: Exterior*** (350, 10 guineas)
594 mm x 809 mm. Proofs before publication line exist.

152 **The Courtyard of the Ducal Palace,** Venice* (250, 4 guineas)
508 mm x 333 mm. Proofs before publication line exist.

153 **Ca'd'oro, Venice** (150, 4 guineas)
Some aquatint, 289 mm x 396 mm (A).

154 **An Old Wharf, Venice**
207 mm x 267 mm.

155 **Palazzo Contarini degli Scrigni** [Venice]
234 mm x 158 mm (A). Possibly the 'On The Grand Canal', RE, 1901 No. 189.

156 **In Northern Spain**
105 mm x 172 mm (A). Based on Escosia (? Ascotia). Possibly a misdating by Armstrong for No. 142 as Hood dates 'In Northern Spain' to 1895.

157 **Rialto** (150, 4 guineas)
394 mm x 279 mm (H).

158 **Gloria Deo In Excelsis – A Christmas Card – The Christ Child Over Uppsala**
76 mm x 110 mm.

1899

159 **The Madonna with a Musket, St Mark's*** (250, 3 guineas)
408 mm x 286 mm.

160 **The Chapel of the Sacrament, St Mark's*** (250, 3 guineas)
408 mm x 286 mm. Proofs before publication line exist.

161 **The Chapel of St Clement, St Mark's*** (250, 3 guineas)
281 mm x 353 mm.

162 **The Baptistry, St Mark's*** (250, 3 guineas)
377 mm x 254 mm.
Stronghold, RE, 1899, No. 43. See No. 113.

1900

163 **Notre Dame, Paris*** (350, 8 guineas)
566 mm x 788 mm.

164 **Barcelona Cathedral: Interior*** (350, 5 guineas)
556 mm x 380 mm. Proofs before publication line exist.

165 **Windsor Castle**

178 mm x 253 mm. 150 proofs with H. Virtue's publication line were published before the plate appeared in the *Art Journal.*

166 **St Elizabeth of Hungary**
172 mm x 127 mm (A).

167 **The Star of Bethlehem – A Christmas Card**
Mentioned in Armstrong, p. 167. See also No. 205.

1901

Fellahah
See No. 100.

168 **Cefalu Cathedral** (350, 8 guineas)
716 mm x 464 mm.

169 **Amiens – Exterior***
375 mm x 556 mm, later cut to 378 mm x 283 mm (A). Both states bear the publication line, but earlier states of both exist.

170 **Balmoral**
175 mm x 253 mm. Proofs exist with H. Virtue's publication line. Printed before the plate was used in the *Art Journal.*

171 **On the River Dee**
279 mm x 203 mm (H).

172 **Buckingham Palace**
176 mm x 253 mm. Proofs exist with H. Virtue's publication line, printed before the plate was used in the *Art Journal.*

173 **Linlithgow – Seen across the Lake**
177 mm x 256 mm. Proofs exist with H. Virtue's publication line printed before the plate was used in the *Art Journal.*
Plaza de la Constitucion: Seville
See No. 57.

173a **On The Grand Canal**
RE, 1901, No. 189. Possibly Nos. 11 or 155.

174 **Angels: Unity Is Strength**
Tondo 6″ diameter 153 mm x 153 mm.
Stockholm
See No. 175.

1902

175 **Stockholm – The Harbour, Ships on the Left**
219 mm x 378 mm. Misdated to 1901 by Armstrong. Possibly in two states.

176 **San Zeno, Verona*** (350, 6 guineas)
398 mm x 536 mm.

177 **Ulm Cathedral*** (5 guineas)
555 mm x 369 mm (A). Armstrong claims that 250 proofs were issued, but Dunthorne's catalogue of 1908 says 175.

178 **Westminster Abbey – The Altar**
267 mm x 184 mm. Proofs exist with H. Virtue's publication line printed before the plate was used in the *Art Journal.*

179 **Burgos Cathedral, North Porch**
With light aquatint, 203 mm x 289 mm. An earlier unfinished proof was in the Hood sale and was dated to 1898 but it was exhibited RE, 1896, No. 24.

180 **Porta San Pietro, Assisi**
172 mm x 121 mm (A).

1903

181 **Westminster Abbey, North Porch** (350, 8 guineas)
721 mm x 533 mm (A).

182 **Assisi: October Evening** (200, 8 guineas)
478 mm x 609 mm.

183 **The Church of St Francis, Assisi** (300, 8 guineas)
483 mm x 609 mm (A).

184 **The Castle of Vitré**
249 mm x 358 mm.

185 **Strasburg** (150, 3 guineas)
337 mm x 219 mm (A).

1904

186 **La Madeleine, Troyes*** (250, 6 guineas)
600 mm x 403 mm. Proofs before publication line exist.
Stockholm
See No. 79.

187 **The Palatine Chapel, Palermo*** (350, 8 guineas)
689 mm x 459 mm.

188 **Palermo, Piazza Garraffa**
292 mm x 200 mm (H).

189 **The Towers of Laon** (150, 4 guineas)
260 mm x 381 mm (A). 260 mm x 402 mm (D).

190 **St Christopher and the Christ Child – A Christmas Card**
125 mm x 198 mm.

1905

191 **York Minster*** (350, 6 guineas)
586 mm x 385 mm. Trial proofs and proofs before publication line exist.

192 **Bayonne** (150, 3 guineas)
422 mm x 262 mm.

193 **Nassauer Haus: Nuremberg** (150, 1 guinea)
203 mm x 130 mm (A).

194 **Capilla del Condestable, Burgos Cathedral**
198 mm x 129 mm. Published in the large paper edition of Armstrong's *Axel Haig and his work* (1905). Unknown limitation.

195 **Portico del Gloria, Santiago de Campostella*** (350, 8 guineas)
676 mm x 453 mm.

196 **Leon**
368 mm x 521 mm.

1906

197 **Copenhagen**
174 mm x 134 mm (B).

198 **Courtyard, Chartres** (150, 1½ guineas)
165 mm x 226 mm (H).

199 **Public Buildings near a Park**
98 mm x 146 mm (H).

200 **St Jerome Cloister, Belem, Lisbon*** (350, 8 guineas)
676 mm x 456 mm. Trial proofs, one touched, and proofs before publication line exist.

201 **Angelès** (150, 2 guineas)
With aquatint, 272 mm x 368 mm. Trial proofs exist.

202 **Burgos: Altar of S. Anna**
RE, 1906, No. 91.

203 **Santa Cruz, Coimbra** (150, 3 guineas)
432 mm x 279 mm (H).

204 **Busaco, Portugal** (150, 4 guineas)
402 mm x 281 mm.

205 **The Star of Bethlehem – A Christmas Card**
Aquatint, 76 mm x 114 mm (H). Hood says this was the Christmas card for both 1900 and 1906, presumably with a change of date.

1907

206 **Montmajour, near Arles** (150, 2 guineas)
203 mm x 305 mm (H).

207 **Ghent*** (150, 6 guineas)
442 mm x 584 mm (B).

208 **In the Cloister Garden**
346 mm x 212 mm. Burgos.

209 **The Château De Vitré** (150, 5 guineas)
749 mm x 356 mm.

210 **Entrance to the Cloisters, Burgos – A Carved Baptism over the Door**
471 mm x 333 mm. Trial proofs exist.
211 **South Aisle, Burgos*** (400, 8 guineas)
688 mm x 453 mm.
212 **Monreale Cathedral*** (325, 8 guineas)
682 mm x 456 mm.

1908

213 **Bayeux**
437 mm x 565 mm. Trial proofs exist.
214 **Toledo Interior – A Procession Approaching** (250, 6 guineas)
594 mm x 399 mm.
215 **Northern Museum, Stockholm** (150, 1½ guineas)
163 mm x 245 mm.
216 **Canterbury Cathedral and Town*** (200, 5 guineas)
428 mm x 610 mm. Trial proofs exist.
217 **Hoar Cross, Chapel of the Holy Trinity** (200, 6 guineas)
596 mm x 396 mm. Trial proofs exist.
218 **North Chancel, Amiens*** (300, 6 guineas)
596 mm x 403 mm. Trial proofs and proofs before publication line exist.
219 **Nuremburg – Seen across Roofs**
350 mm x 449 mm.
220 **Ruins of St Nicholas, Wisby**
164 mm x 218 mm.
221 **St Lo, Normandy**
432 mm x 584 mm (H).
222 **St Anastasia, Verona** (150, 4 guineas)
568 mm x 397 mm.

1909

223 **Segovia, Spain – A Street Scene**
184 mm x 130 mm (H). According to Hood's catalogue this was started in 1886 but finished in 1909.
224 **Burgos, East Ambulatory*** (150, 5 guineas)
16½″ x 11″, 419 mm x 296 mm. Proofs before publication line exist.
225 **Pena Castle, Cintra, Portugal**
591 mm x 393 mm.
226 **Pulpit, Palma*** (200, 6 guineas)
393 mm x 541 mm.
227 **Salamanca – Cross and Cathedral Beyond*** (150, 6 guineas)
579 mm x 368 mm.
228 **Town by a River**
247 mm x 172 mm (H).

229 **Auch, South France**
RE, 1909, No. 174. (Small).

1910

230 **South Aisle Looking West, Burgos Cathedral*** (300, 8 guineas)
716 mm x 488 mm.
231 **Chartres – A Bend in a Stream** (150)
184 mm x 248 mm (H).
232 **Antwerp, Place St Nicholas** (100, 2 guineas)
276 mm x 197 mm.
233 **Toledo, View of the South Aisle*** (400, 8 guineas)
715 mm x 487 mm. Proofs before publication line exist.

1911

234 **Castle Gierstein** (150, 4 guineas)
530 mm x 362 mm.
235 **Scaligeri Monuments, Verona** (250, 4 guineas)
505 mm x 345 mm (H).
236 **St Étienne Cathedral, Bourges*** (300, 8 guineas)
417 mm x 571 mm. RA, 1911, No. 1382. Proofs before publication line exist.
237 **South Transept, St Mark's*** (350, 6 guineas)
441 mm x 568 mm.

1912

238 **Canterbury – Tower Through Trees**
444 mm x 308 mm (B). RA, 1912, No. 1501.
239 **St Ours, Loches**
245 mm x 170 mm. A proof inscribed 'Trial Proof No. 1' has been seen.
240 **Choir Screen, South Aisle, Amiens** (250, 4 guineas)
257 mm x 448 mm. Trial proofs exist.
241 **Christ Church, Boston** (80)
Some aquatint, 144 mm x 112 mm. Published by Iconographic Society of Boston, Series II, No. 4.
242 **Niedpath Castle, Scotland**
RE, 1912, No. 143.

1913

243 **Belfry of Bruges**
547 mm x 338 mm. Trial proofs exist. RA, 1915, No. 234.

244 **Cologne Cathedral: Interior** (250, 5 guineas)
517 mm x 371 mm. Trial proofs exist.

245 **Lisieux**
679 mm x 530 mm. Trial proofs exist.

246 **On the Dyle, Malines**
356 mm x 533 mm (B).

247 **Palermo Cathedral** (250, 6 guineas)
482 mm x 613 mm. RA, 1913, No. 1519. Trial proofs exist.

248 **Palermo, Monte Pelerino**
483 mm x 718 mm

1914

249 **Campanile, Venice**
533 mm x 372 mm (B). RA, 1914, No. 1180.

250 **Ely Cathedral: Interior**
651 mm x 413 mm (B).

251 **Cairo, Citadel and Tombs of the Mamelukes**
267 mm x 383 mm.

252 **Brig O'Balgownie**
303 mm x 442 mm. Trial proofs exist.

253 **The Cloisters, the Monastery of Batalha, Portugal**
RA, 1914, No. 1182.

1915

254 **Aberdeen**
341 mm x 305 mm.

255 **Toledo: Cathedral and Street Scene**
463 mm x 297 mm (B).

256 **Lourdes – The Pilgrimage Church**
320 mm x 242 mm.

1916

257 **Lourdes – The Castle**
303 mm x 468 mm.

258 **Segovia – Women by a Fountain**
454 mm x 306 mm. Trial proofs exist. RA, 1916, No. 277.

259 **Confidences – At the Fountain, Seville**
591 mm x 366 mm.

260 **Cintra – Seen from the Hills**
195 mm x 245 mm. A proof inscribed '1st Trial' exists.

261 **Zaragoza**
254 mm x 421 mm.

262 **Lisieux Cathedral**
448 mm x 295 mm.

263 **The Cloisters, St Trophimus, Arles**
425 mm x 312 mm.

1917

264 **Alhambra, Spain**
243 mm x 333 mm.

265 **Kalmar Castle, Sweden**
305 mm x 229 mm.

266 **Lisieux – A Street Scene**
464 mm x 308 mm. RA, 1917, No. 1181. Published by W. R. Howell.

1918

267 **Assisi: From the Hotel Subiaco**
277 mm x 371 mm.

268 **Ballater**
311 mm x 511 mm.

269 **Leon Cathedral – In 1875**
371 mm x 526 mm.

270 **Constantinople**
RE, 1918, No. 82.

271 **On the Bosphorus**
RE, 1918, No. 82.

272 **The Rock of Ronda**
RE, 1919, No. 103.

273 **Nuremberg, The Tower of St Lawrence Church**
454 mm x 317 mm.

1919

274 **Kelso**
$11\frac{5}{8}''$ x $17\frac{3}{4}''$, 371 mm x 526 mm. Trial proofs exist.

275 **Salamanca Cathedral**
$14\frac{1}{4}''$ x $21\frac{1}{8}''$, 361 mm x 537 mm. Only an unfinished and unsigned impression seen.

276 **St Gil, Burgos: Capilla De Natividad**
RE, 1920, No. 130.

Undated

277 **Hawker, Mont St Michel**
200 mm x 133 mm.

278 **Morning: a Lake or River and a Twin-spired Cathedral in the Distance**
Almost pure aquatint, 169 mm x 218 mm. There may be two plates of similar size and subject: the Hood sale catalogue describes one with Lombardy pines on the left.

279 **Calm Sea**
Aquatint, 111 mm x 130 mm. Neither signed nor dated in the plate. Possibly No. 109.

280 **Dalhem**
$3\frac{7}{8}''$ x $6''$.

Projected and Probably Unexecuted Etchings

These were subjects exhibited in Haig's 1883 watercolour show and were to be etched at 8 guineas, size about 686 mm x 256 mm.

Toledo Cathedral
Courtyard in Seville, Near the Church of San Salvador
St Juan de los Reyes, Toledo, In the Cloisters
A Street in Fuentarabia
In a Chapel, Burgos Cathedral
In Toledo Cathedral

The first and the last two may have been the basis for smaller prints.

Lithographs

In addition to the plates made for *The Architect* and other magazines Haig made a number of lithographs in the 1890s and later.

L1 **Mrs Haig – Semper Fidelis**
213 mm x 158 mm.

L2 **Sketches at Bruges**
(a) Christ on the Cross. About 102 mm x 178 mm (H).
(b) Count and Countess of Salamanca at an altar. About 102 mm x 178 mm (H).

L3 **Two Studies**
(a) Girl with a pitcher. 245 mm x 184 mm.
(b) Girl winding wool
143 mm x 133 mm.

L4 **La Lonja, Valencia** (185, 1 guinea)

454 mm x 308 mm. This and Nos L5–L10 were exhibited at Dunthorne's exhibition of 'Original Lithographs' in 1895. A reduced state of this print – 205 mm wide and lacking the left hand side – was exhibited at the Paris International Exhibition celebrating the centenary of lithography.

L5 **Durham, 1894**
254 mm x 150 mm. Dated by Hood to 1891.

L6 **Cyclopean Doorway, Tarragona** (1 guinea)
286 mm x 228 mm.

L7 **Cloisters, Gerona** (1 guinea)

L8 **Cairo** (1 guinea)

L9 **Study by Lamplight Mrs Haig** (1 guinea, July 1895)
305 mm x 292 mm. ('Lady Reading by a Lamp')

L10 **Fragment of a Reredos** (½ guinea)

L11 **Church at Gothem, In the Island of Gothland** (1905)

Bibliography

There is no modern, full-length biography of Axel Haig. The following texts formed the starting-point for this study: E. A. Armstrong, *Axel Herman Haig and his Work* (1905); *Svensk Konstnärs Lexikon* iii (1958), pp. 213–5; *Sale Catalogue of the Collection of J. Boland* (American Art Association, New York, 1919); *Sale Catalogue of the R. H. Hood Collection* (American Art Association, New York, 1919); A. Gauffin, 'A. H. Hagg', in *Vvar 8 dag* (1910), no. 13; E. G. Folker, 'En Etsning af A. H. Hagg', in *Ord och bild* (1897), pp. 191–2; *Svenskt Biografiskt Lexikon* xix (1969).

For the artistic context of Haig's career, see W. Burges, 'Architectural Drawing' *RIBA Papers* (1860–61), pp. 15–23; M. B. Adams, 'Architectural Drawings', *RIBA Journal* N.S.I. (1884–5), pp. 111–8, 128; R. Blomfield, *Architectural Drawing and Draughtsmanship* (1912); T. Simpson, *Modern Etchings* (1919); F. Newbolt, *History of the Royal Society of Painter-Etchers and Engravers* (1930); J. Mordaunt Crook, *William Burges and the High Victorian Dream* (1981).

Detailed references to contemporary papers and journals are cited in the footnotes.

Index

Figures in square brackets refer to print numbers; figures in **bold** refer to plate numbers.

1 Axel Herman Haig (1835–1921): 'The Piranesi of the Gothic Revival'.

2 Axel Haig dressed as a Viking in 1898, for a fancy dress party given by Conan Doyle. (Photo: Private collection).

Burges in medieval dress.
hoto: National Portrait Gallery).

4 William Burges (1827–81).
(*The Graphic* 1881)

5 Grayshurst, Haslemere, Surrey (1891). Haig's Christmas card for 1892 [116] etching of the house he designed for himself.

6 Ferniehurst, Jedburgh, Scotland; scheme for restoration: a watercolour (1872) by Axel Haig. (Private collection).

7 Fantasy Castle: a watercolour by Axel Haig (n.d.). (Private collection).

8 Saint Simeon Stylites by W. Burges (1860). (*Building News* xxvi, 1874, 413).

9 Cardiff Castle: Burges's unfinished scheme for the Great Staircase. Watercolour (1874) by Axel Haig. (Private collection).

10 Cardiff Castle: Burges's Winter Smoking Room in Lord Bute's Clock Tower, Watercolour (1870) by Axel Haig. (National Trust, Knightshayes, Devon).

11 Cardiff Castle: Burges's 'Swiss' Bridge. From a perspective (1879) by Axel Haig. (*The Architect*, xxi, 1879, p. 281).

12 Cardiff Castle: Lord Bute's Study in Burges's Bute Tower. From a perspective (1879) by Axel Haig. (*The Architect*, xxi, 1879, p. 89).

13 House for James McConnochie, Park Place, Cardiff: Burges's executed design. From a perspective (1872) by Axel Haig. (*The Architect* xxvii, 1882, 221).

14 Law Courts, London, Strand front: Burges's competition design. From a perspective (1866) by Axel Haig. (*Building News*, xiv, 1867, p. 306).

15 Knightshayes, Devon: Burges's executed design. From a perspective (1870) by Axel Haig. (*The Architect*, xxvii, 1882, p. 221).

16 Speech Room, Harrow School: Burges's original scheme. From a perspective by Axel Haig (1871). (*The Architect*, xxvii, 1882, p. 221).

17 Speech Room, Harrow School: Burges's design for the interior. From a perspective (1871) by Axel Haig. (*The Architect*, xxvii, 1882, p. 221).

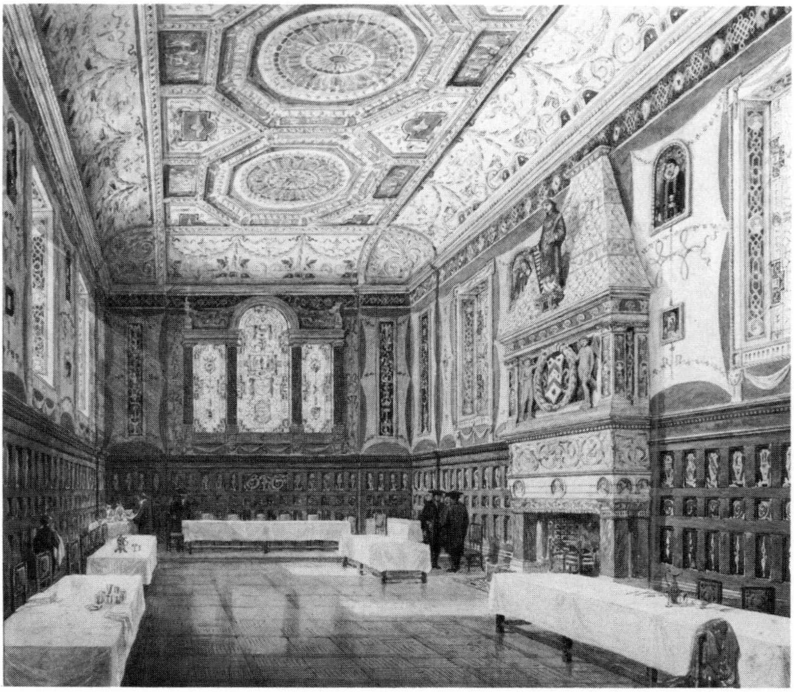

18 Worcester College, Oxford: Burges's scheme for the hall. Watercolour (1873) by Axel Haig. (Worcester College, Oxford).

19 St Mary's Cathedral, Edinburgh: Burges's competition design. Watercolour (1873) by Axel Haig. (Private collection).

20 St Mary's Cathedral, Edinburgh: interior. From a perspective (1873) by Axel Haig. (*Builder*, xxiv, 1873, p. 227).

21 St Finbar's Cathedral, Cork: Burges's Bishop's Throne. Watercolour (1877) by Axel Haig. (RIBA).

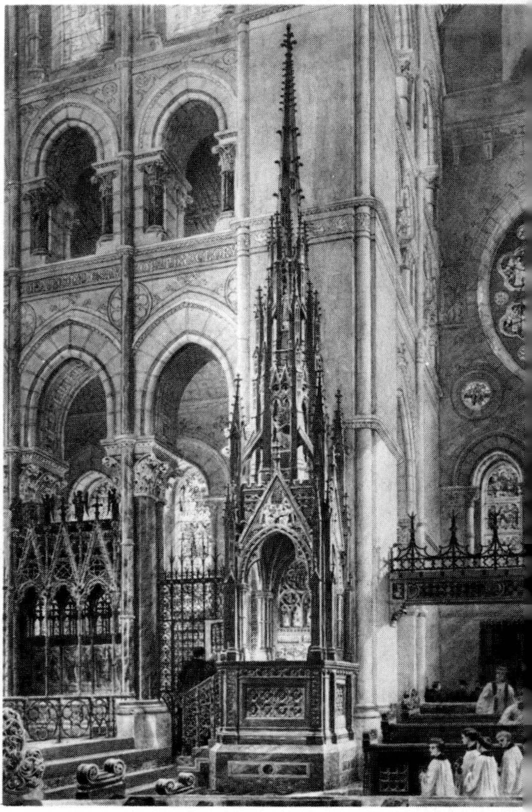

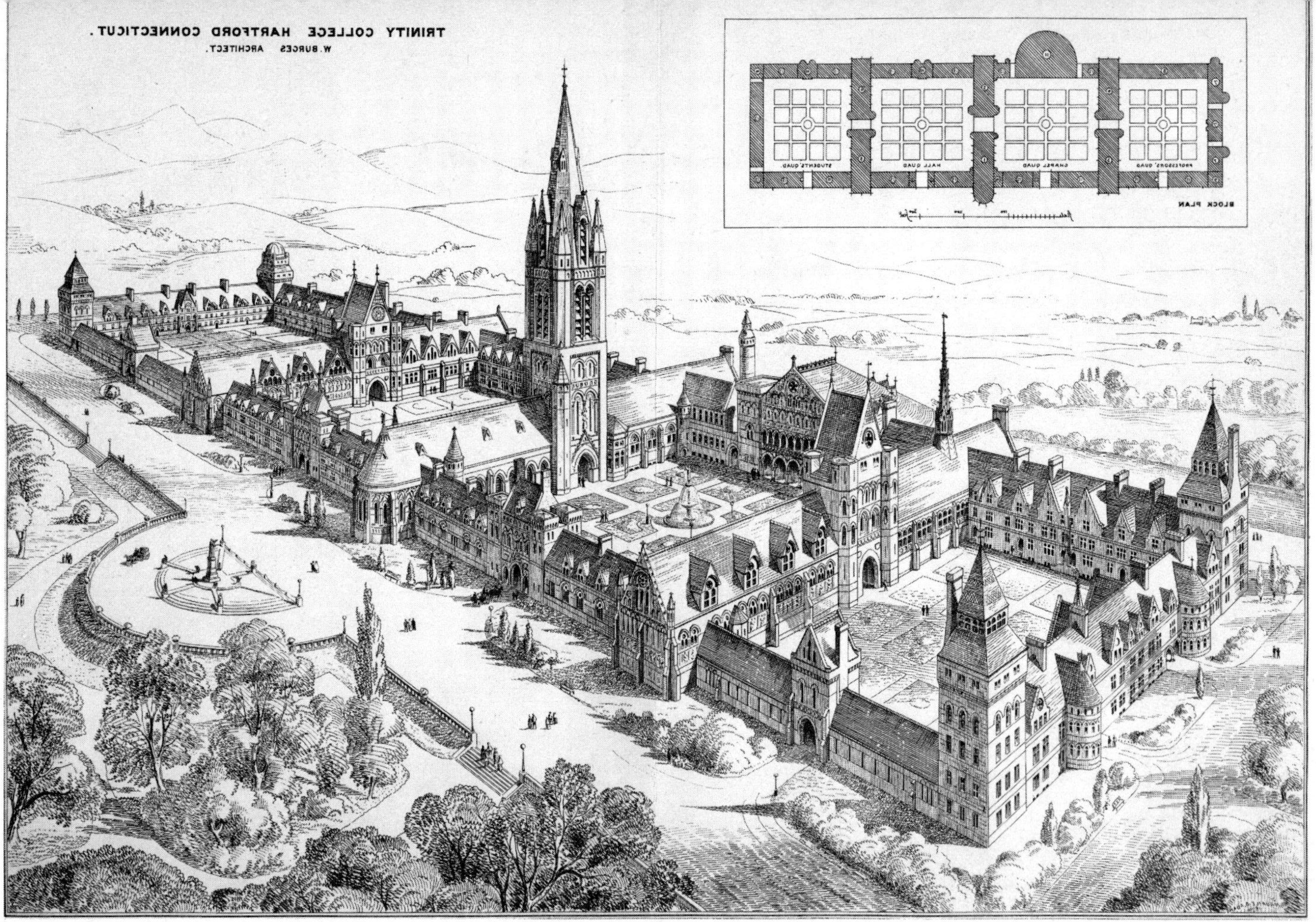

22 Trinity College, Hartford, Connecticut, USA: Burges's prospective scheme. From a perspective (1873) by Axel Haig.

23 St Mary the Virgin, Studley Royal, Yorkshire: Burges's chancel. From a perspective (1874) by Axel Haig. (*The Architect*, xi, 1874, 346).

24 Tower House, Melbury Road, Kensington: Burges's library. From a perspective (1880) by Axel Haig. (*The Architect*, xxiii, 1880, p. 314).

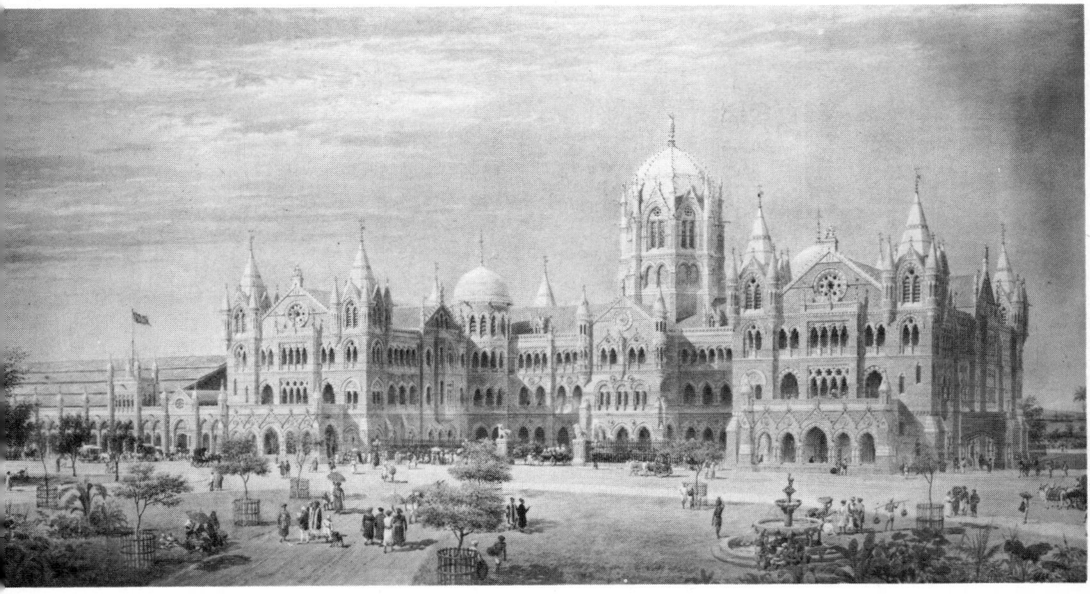

25 Victoria Railway Terminus, Bombay: architect F. W. Stevens. Watercolour by Axel Haig (1880). (India Office Library).

26 St Paul's Cathedral, London: Burges's scheme for interior decoration. Watercolour (1874) by Axel Haig. (Private collection).

27 'The Vesper Bell' (1879) [18] Based on Nuremburg. (National Museum, Stockholm).

28 'Caen: Tower of St Pierre' (1879) [20].

29 'Flemish Lace Workers' (1879) [22]. At Bruges.

30 'The Morning of the Festival' (1880) [24]. Based on Bruges.

31 'A Quiet Hour' (1880) [25]. Based on Chartres.

32 'An Old German Mill' (1880) [26]. Based on Luneburg.

33 'At Haddon Hall' (1880) [28]. The elopement of Dorothy Vernon.(?)

34 'Uppsala: Design for the Restoration of the Cathedral' (1881) [32].

35 'Mont St Michel' (1882) [35].

36 'Chartres: Street Scene and Cathedral' (1882) [37].

37 'Peterborough Cathedral' (1883) [42].

38 'An Old Hanse Town' (1883) [45]. Based on Hamburg.

39 ‘Uppsala Cathedral: Design for the Completion of the Interior’ (1884) [47].

40 'The Fountain of St George' (1885) [54]. Based on Rothenburg, Bavaria.

41 'Westminster Abbey: Entrance to the Poets' Corner' (1885) [60].

42 'Plaza de la Constitucion, Seville' (1886) [57].

43 'Limburg on the Lahn' (1886) [62].

44 'The Alcazar, Segovia' (1886) [63].

45 'Schloss Zwingenburg' (1886) [65].

46 'Cologne, Night Effect' (1886) [66].

47 ‘Pampeluna, Returning from the Fair’ (1887) [67].

48 'L'Eglise des Dominicains, Arles' (1887) [68].

49 'Stockholm: The Floating Market' (1888) [74].

50 'Burgos: Interior' (1888) [80].

58 'Assisi: October Evening' (1903) [182].

57 'The Legend of the Bells' (1895) [141].

55 'Castle Nowhere' (1892) [113]. (National Museum, Stockholm).

54 'The Portals of Rheims Cathedral' (1892) [110].

53 'Wisby: Towing in the Prize' (1891) [104].

52 'In the Arab Quarter, Cairo' (1891) [102].

51 'Wisby: Morning', or 'The Walk by the Shore' (1888) [88].

59 'The Castle of Vitré' (1903) [184].

60 'The Palatine Chapel, Palermo' (1904) [187].

61 'Portico del Gloria, Santiago de Compostella' (1905) [195].

62 'St Jerome Cloister, Belem, Lisbon' (1906) [200].

63 'Busaco, Portugal' (1906) [204].

64 ‘Monreale Cathedral’ (1907) [212].